10 Strategies to Avoid Regrets

GETTING IT
RIGHT

The Generational Impact of
Our Life & Estate Plan

10 Strategies to Avoid Regrets

GETTING IT RIGHT

The Generational Impact of Our Life & Estate Plan

Gary Bottoms

BOOKLOGIX®
Alpharetta, Georgia

Alpharetta, Georgia

The cases presented are applicable to the individuals depicted and may not be representative of the experience of others. The testimonials are not paid and are not indicative of the future performance of success.

This material was created to provide accurate and reliable information on the subjects covered but should not be regarded as a complete analysis of these subjects. It is not intended to provide specific legal, tax or other professional advice. The services of an appropriate professional should be sought regarding your individual situation.

Any guarantees offered by life insurance products are subject to the claims-paying ability of the issuing insurance company. There are considerable issues that need to be considered before replacing life insurance such as, but not limited to; commissions, fees, expenses, surrender charges, premiums, and new contestability period. There may also be unfavorable tax consequences caused by surrendering an existing policy, such as a potential tax on outstanding policy loans. Please discuss your situation with your financial advisor.

To ensure compliance with requirements imposed by the IRS, we inform you that any U.S. federal tax advice contained in this document is not intended or written to be used, and cannot be used, for the purpose of (i) avoiding penalties under the Internal Revenue Code, or (ii) promoting, marketing, or recommending to another party any transaction matter addressed herein.

Copyright © 2013 by Gary T. Bottoms
Hardcover edition November 2013

ISBN: 978-1-61005-426-3

Unless otherwise noted, scripture is derived from THE HOLY BIBLE, NEW INTERNATIONAL VERSION®, NIV® Copyright © 1973, 1978, 1984, 2011 by Biblica, Inc.® Used by permission. All rights reserved worldwide.

Printed in the United States of America

♾ This paper meets the requirements of ANSI/NISO Z39.48-1992 (Permanence of Paper)

My parents

Harold Bottoms (May 9, 1923 – January 29, 2013)

and

Mary Bottoms (February 15, 1927 – June 15, 2007)

Whose Impact Is Continuing

My wife and life partner

Melissa Bottoms

Who Is Always an Encourager

My adult children

David Bottoms, Jonathan Bottoms, and Laura Higginbotham

Who Are the Future

People with extraordinary privilege have complex challenges to define, accept, and meet.

What we do or don't do can affect not only us, but maybe two or three succeeding generations as well, possibly more.

CONTENTS

Part III
A Place to Begin

FOREWORD

My father always taught me that luck was when opportunity meets preparation. It should also be said that peace of mind comes when life's inevitable tragedies are met by thoughtful preparation. Gary Bottoms' book, *Getting It Right*, demonstrates how to prepare for both life's opportunities and tragedies.

As a businessman and public servant, I have met many successful people who have accumulated wealth, and I have seen a lot of them lose it. The difference in those who kept their wealth and those that did not was their preparation for life's unknowns. None of us know if or when death, disability, disease, separation, or opportunity may come our way, but if we are not prepared, our financial fate and that of our loved ones could fall into the hands of others.

Many people become introspective when discussing business succession or end of life decisions. As *Getting It Right* demonstrates, assembling a team of professionals to plan with you, and then assist when the time comes to execute the plan, makes all the difference in the world.

There is an old story of the wise man being confronted by a young boy who is clasping a baby bird in his hands. The young boy asks, "Mister, if you are so wise please tell me, is the baby bird in my hands alive or dead?" The wise man paused, knowing if he said the bird was alive the boy could crush the bird, or if he said the bird was dead the boy could open his hands and let the bird live. So the wise man answered, "Young man, the fate of that bird is up to you."

So it is with *Getting It Right*. It is up to you.

– Johnny Isakson
United States Senator

ACKNOWLEDGMENTS

I n 1975, I began the journey to learn the things I'm sharing with you in this book. Over the years, I've been blessed to meet and work with many wonderful people from whom I've learned so much. The stories in this book were gleaned from those experiences. My commitment to client privacy is paramount and prevents me from identifying individuals, but please know that I am indebted to each of you.

I'm grateful to a number of friends who have encouraged me and offered insight as this book was being written. Their openness about the reasons why and how to do estate planning were an inspiration.

I wish to thank: Tommy Allegood, Ralph Antolino, Diane Baker, Micky Blackwell, Tim Bradigan, Bernie Brown, Doug Chaffins, Russ Crosson, Bill Dean, Lori Evers, Jim Fleming, Larry Freeman, Rick Hamilton, Robin Hensley, Roger Hines, Mike Hoffman, Jack Kennedy, Bob Kiser, Jim Moye, Brian Nygaard, Bryan Owens, Floyd Propst, Tim Sheehan, Stanley M. Smith, Barry St. Clair, Dan Sullivan, Tony Turner, Jim Underwood, Ann Watkins, Jay Whorton, and Tom Wright.

INTRODUCTION

Why We Matter

In addition to financial wealth, I believe most family leaders want to create a legacy of meaning that lives on and continues to following generations. The meaning that I'm referring to is deep and in many ways silent, but it's significant.

When our children were in their teens, Melissa and I made a strategic decision to take David, Jonathan and Laura to Europe, one at a time. David's trip included Vienna, Austria. I recall standing inside a cathedral that was about a thousand years old as he pointed to a foreign looking inscription near the ceiling. He called upon his knowledge of Latin and read the words: *"He who finds me, finds life."*

As we stood there looking up toward the ceiling, I recall thinking two things: first, I would've never been able to read that. And second, I wonder what life was like for whoever inscribed the words a thousand years earlier. I later discovered that the inscription is from Proverbs 8:35.

That person's life was certainly much different from ours, but it was the one life they had to live. Their life ended a long time ago. They passed on—yet something was left behind. That's the way it has happened for every generation. Ours will be no different. That's why we matter.

Walk with me through this book, and I'll share with you some things that I've observed and I'm learning.

I believe our actions and omissions don't merely speak louder than our words—sometimes they echo into future generations. Patterns tend to persist.

For my family, my guess is that, a couple of generations ago, no one was giving much thought to what would be going on several decades into the future. But, in recent years I've been thinking through how our lives have evolved from a relationship and financial standpoint.

Though I'm not preoccupied with the past, I've thought about what has transpired over the last several decades. I've become motivated to consider how what I do now fits into the grand scheme of things going forward into the future.

This book focuses on what I've discovered. Those discoveries fall into two broad categories: relationships and estate planning, with a bent toward life insurance planning—my specialty.

Most of us are driven by an instinct that wants to prevent bad things from happening. This is why we lock our doors at night, follow the maintenance schedules for our automobiles, and avoid high places with no rails. From a family legacy, financial security, and estate-planning standpoint, this book is oriented around helping the reader avoid ten regrets that most would consider to be unacceptable.

An "unacceptable regret" is a painful result that occurs at the end of our lifetime, or for others after we are gone that, with intentional planning, could have been prevented.

I've observed that most of our clients really do wish to avoid allowing, or worse, causing financial harm or relationship damage to those they love the most. For those who have passed on and failed, if they could've seen into the future and observed what was going to take place, I believe most would've taken extraordinary steps to "get it right."

The real-life stories included in this book illustrate ten strategies that are based upon my experiences. Following the stories, regrets that could've been avoided and regrets that actually happened are identified. However, the names and enough of the details have been changed in order to protect the confidentiality of those involved. As you read the accounts of these real lives, please notice that multiple individuals were impacted in each situation. I will walk us through a process oriented towards doing our best to "get it right."

The echo of what one generation does follows to succeeding generations. That's sobering to think about because so much of the future is not under our control. But we can make a difference in the lives of others by making wise decisions and plans that increase our chances of "getting it right." *It* being the impact of our lives, what we do and don't do for and with others.

By the way, "getting it right" does not imply perfection.

Ironically, being a perfectionist may go hand-in-hand with being a procrastinator—an enemy of the process that I will describe. We can make a best effort based upon what we know and what we have to work with. Plans usually evolve over time and the objective may be a moving target.

Having assets and possessions creates important responsibilities. I've observed over my career that for many of our clients their wealth has accumulated slowly. Often they don't realize the complexity that has been created and what their responsibilities are to handle it.

It may be that they struggled financially in the past and remember how it felt. They know what it's like to struggle financially and they never want to go there again.

They are nervous about making plans and possibly letting go because it all seems complicated and there are many options to consider. Making plans seems so final. As a result, maybe no plans are made. On a basic level, they would really like to have direction and confidence oriented around a process to accomplish their objectives.

Since 1975, we have seen much that has gone well with estate planning, and we've seen results that were disappointing due to lack of planning. We've observed financial hardship and dysfunctional relationships that could've been prevented.

The purpose of the following pages is to move you toward planning for the future and take a look at what can happen. I hope it will stimulate your thinking, give you direction and create confidence. I want to help you explore the reasons "why" making the investment in planning to "get it right" makes sense, and provide a look at what that process might look like.

What we do or don't do really does matter.

MY FAMILY'S STORY

In 1929, my grandfather, Homer Bottoms, tragically took his own life. Just prior to ending his life, he made eye contact with his six-year-old son who later became my father. All families have stories, good and not so good, and I invite you to continue reading as I share a little of my own family's story.

I don't know what led to my grandfather's decision to take his life, but my guess is that it developed slowly over a long period of time. I do know for sure that it had a significant effect on my father who, as far as I know, never discussed that day or what he witnessed with anyone until about sixty years later.

Often the really big things in life evolve rather slowly and are sometimes unseen, but they can be the most impactful.

My grandfather's death began a chain of events that continue to have an effect today. For starters, he left a young thirty-year-old widow, Laura Bottoms, with four young children to raise during the Great Depression. They had no choice but to leave their home in Talking Rock, Georgia, and move in with my great-grandparents, Jim and Maggie Southerland, who had a small home on Marble Mill Road in Marietta, Georgia, where my great-grandfather worked at the marble mill.

This relocation in 1929 is the reason I was born in Marietta and still make my home there today. Marietta is where I met Melissa, my wife, and where our three grown children now reside.

My grandfather worked for the railroad in North Georgia and as a result had life insurance. I don't know the amount of coverage, but it was enough to allow my grandmother to purchase, in 1937, forty acres in West Cobb County for $700. She lived on and farmed this property, in some fashion, for the rest of her life until she passed away at age eighty-seven.

Her life wasn't easy. She raised four emotionally healthy children during the depression and lost one of her sons in combat during World War II. As I was growing up, I noticed how much her remaining three adult children adored her.

Although my dad never discussed it, I suspect that his mother's real world experience with life insurance was one of the reasons he chose the life insurance business as his profession. Furthermore, I know that indirectly this was one of the reasons that her grandson (me) chose the insurance and financial security business as his profession.

Following my grandmother's death, the property in West Cobb County was sold and the proceeds were divided among her surviving children. The proceeds from the sale were not a fortune. But, as it turned out, the financial resources that began with life insurance in 1929 provided significant financial help during the final years of my parent's lives eight decades later. Both of my parents suffered from Alzheimer's disease and needed continuous and expensive care for eight years.

On his good days, after my mother passed away, my father spoke openly about joining her in heaven and of his love for his family. It was a blessing to be a part of those conversations that I'll never forget. At the end of my parents' lives, it was clear that significant attention had been given to personal relationships and planning.

My father eventually overcame the emotional trauma that he suffered as a young boy. He was healed. He understood the impact that his life, actions and words would have on those around him.

He overcame a lot and understood the importance of "getting it right."

– Gary Bottoms

PART I

THE SOUL OF PLANNING

LOVE AND AVOIDABLE REGRETS

"For every thousand hacking at the leaves of evil there is one striking at the root."

– Henry David Thoreau

The phrase "soul of planning" paints a word picture in my mind. *Soul* implies something that lives on. It's vital, deep, and possibly silent, but ever-present. It's an undercurrent that influences our decisions and motivates us to care deeply about how our actions affect others around us. *Planning* includes a thought process that leads to a predetermined destination. The root of the thought process and the resulting plans for generational impact is love.

Judge Floyd Propst retired a few years ago after serving for twenty-five years as the elected probate judge for Fulton County, which includes Atlanta, Georgia. During those years, he presided over family disputes involving almost every issue imaginable. He now has a private law practice with a focus upon family probate issues. He's seen a lot.

Judge Propst and I are friends, and I've learned from what he's shared with me about his past experiences, which have been many. During one of our conversations, I asked him what his most significant observation might be after many years of presiding over family disputes. He thought for a moment and then he looked at me and said, "It comes down to love."

If love is in the mix, the imperfections may be overcome and the family will be able to work things out. So love is the one ingredient that can overcome. If love is present, it can become the "root" that holds everything else together.

A poignant moment occurred during one of the judge's cases involving the settlement of a parent's estate between two siblings. Both siblings were in their mid-fifties and successful in their own right. One was a surgeon, and the other was an attorney. When the two parties finally faced one another in court, one of the siblings took the stand and turned to the other and said, "Mother always loved you the most." After the death of a parent or loved one, old hurts and childlike feelings thought to be healed and buried can resurface.

It's been said that money and possessions can bring out the worst in human beings. The judge shared a true story that is amusing but sad. It's not a story about love; it's a story about greed.

A lonely, elderly lady who didn't have a husband or children was fearful of being alone during her last years. She had three inattentive nieces and craved their attention and affection.

So she created a will and shared the contents with them. Her will indicated that she was planning to leave her oil wells in Oklahoma to one niece, her condominium in New York City to another, and her yacht in Miami to the third niece. This was the motivation the nieces needed. During her final years, the three nieces became very attentive and showed lots of affection toward their aging aunt.

However, about six months after her death, her executor appeared in court to declare that the assets could not be found. It was later determined that the assets did not exist. The aunt had simply created an atmosphere that provided the companionship she longed to have. Yes, these things do happen.

Estate planning is a mix of emotional, psychological, financial, and legal ingredients. Yes, life insurance is frequently a critical part of the plan. It creates cash for the support of survivors, payment of debts, taxes, business obligations, and many other needs. But, getting it right involves more.

The "more" that I'm speaking of refers to the proper legal documents, the income, and estate tax aspects of the plan, along with the interpersonal and business relationships that are involved.

The core purpose of the entire plan is to accomplish our client's thoroughly considered objectives. I'm referring to not only the objectives upon death that involve the settlement of an estate, but the objectives beyond that, which may have an impact upon the heirs for years to come.

We may want our accumulated resources to be used in ways that help people and causes that we care about, provide protection for those that may be harmed by our death, and possibly above all else, do no harm. An unintended consequence of a financially successful life, usually accompanied by lots of hard work, may be the creation of an environment that harms those whom we care about the most.

I believe that human beings are, by nature, made to desire relationships with others. Spending time alone is important, but most of us really do enjoy and want to interact with others in a connected and transparent way. Some give it up and retreat into the high mountains and live as hermits, but way down deep, I believe they wish their lifestyles were different and include meaningful relationships.

Estate planning at its core is about others. Financial planning involves lots of objectives like saving for retirement, minimizing taxes, making plans for future purchases, and so forth. But estate planning is primarily about what happens with your possessions and the ongoing effect of your wealth on others after you're gone. It is about what happens with all of your accumulated assets. It involves your large and valuable items as well as everything else you own including personal property. Your jewelry and items around your home may not have much financial value, but might represent an emotional attachment to you and be very important to someone in your life.

On another level, estate planning is thinking through the perhaps unfinished projects and obligations that may be present when your time comes to die. It's about creating provisions for needs that you would've met had you lived on. It's about avoiding unintended consequences and unacceptable regrets.

Most of us know what financial insecurity feels like. A few years ago, many of our clients felt that they were set for life because of their retirement plan, their accumulated reserves, and a good business environment. However, we have been reminded that business cycles do occur and the prosperity curve does not always trend upward. Things can and do change.

Some who thought they were forever past being financially concerned about the future have become more conservative in recent years. Those who have regained financial stability after experiencing the stress of cash flow problems, and maybe too much debt, never want to go back.

There is a renewed interest in being prepared for surprises and planning for unforeseen risks, both for ourselves as well as those that we love. Paying attention to the important but not necessarily urgent details of our financial lives has grown in popularity.

For most, leaving a legacy of stress, resentment, conflict, or confusion behind would be an unacceptable regret. Or, to say it differently, this would be an unintended consequence of a life that outwardly appeared to be quite successful.

An Unintended Consequence of Success

Melissa and I, along with a group of friends, toured Napa Valley, California. The Robert Mondavi winery was among several wineries that we visited.

This is one of the most respected wineries in the world, and the tour guide told an interesting story. As she told it, Robert Mondavi smacked his brother Peter twice in the face, hard, in front of their mother. The brothers were in their fifties at the time, and the setting was a big family gathering at the winery that was supposed to be a happy, festive occasion. The conflict erupted about six years following their dad's death in 1959.

Their dad had founded the family wine business and when he died, he left control of the corporation in the hands of their mother who had no experience in the business. She was simply unable to handle all of the complexities of managing a business, much less a family business. The elder Mr. Mondavi left an overriding directive related to the continuation of the business: Robert and Peter would run the business together.

The brothers did not agree on much, and as long as the father was around, he would step in and settle disputes as they happened. But, as noted above, the siblings did not get along. Ultimately, after the father's death, a meltdown occurred and it became obvious that the plan wasn't working.

Robert was thrown out of the family's winery and a long, ugly, and costly legal battle followed. This outcome, I am sure, would have been unacceptable to the senior Mr. Mondavi. Robert later struck out on his own and became very successful, but this story is an example of how family-owned businesses and family-owned assets can lead to serious and lasting disagreements.

This story is a word picture of an unintended consequence of business success. The events slowly evolved, but undoubtedly, the father would have preferred a different outcome. It is likely that he would have found the ultimate outcome of his business dream and his family relationships to be an unacceptable regret. At the end of the day, brotherly love is high on a parent's wish list.

None of this should surprise us because interpersonal disagreements have been around forever. Furthermore, there's not much reason for optimism that we will be able to eliminate such problems in the future. On a basic level, about all we can do is control what we do and don't do and minimize the possibility that we are contributing to future problems.

UNACCEPTABLE REGRETS

Pain for the mother, brothers' relationships broken, family lawsuit, and business interests split.

Rivalry: Love Can Trump Anger

I heard a sermon in church related to generational relationships that actually gave me the idea for this book. The story was from the book of Genesis in the Old Testament, and it began in Chapter 25 with the relationship between two brothers, Jacob and Esau.

In summary, Esau, who was the older brother, traded his inheritance rights as the firstborn son to his younger brother Jacob for a pot of soup. He was very hungry. This was a life-altering moment for Jacob, Esau, and generations that followed. It's amazing to think that over 2,000 years later we're thinking through what happened that long ago.

Later in Chapter 27, Jacob tricked their father Isaac into giving him the blessing that rightly should have belonged to Esau because he was the oldest son. When Esau found out about this, he was understandably incensed because his blessing as the older son had been irrevocably given to his younger brother Jacob. The blessing could not be withdrawn. Esau vowed to kill his brother Jacob as soon as his father died.

Jacob's antenna was up and he realized that things were not looking good for him if he stuck around, so he moved away.

Years later, in Chapter 32, Jacob decided to travel along with his large family and many possessions to his brother Esau. In advance, Jacob sent a message to Esau asking for acceptance. In the message, Jacob referred to himself as Esau's servant and referred to Esau as his master. This trip involved significant personal danger and faith, especially when messengers returned and told Jacob that his brother Esau was on the way to meet him. And, he was bringing four hundred men with him.

As the two groups approached each other, Jacob bowed down flat on the ground seven times as he was walking toward his brother Esau. Jacob wanted forgiveness. The good news is that Esau ran to meet Jacob and put his arms around him and hugged him. He could have easily killed him instead. Esau forgave his brother Jacob, and Jacob's son, Joseph, saw all of this happen.

Years later, Joseph had the opportunity to either kill his brothers or forgive them because they had sold him into slavery. He chose to forgive. He did what he saw his uncle Esau do for his father.

We are, in part, who we are because of those that came before us and we make decisions that will shape the lives of those that follow us.

In this story, the older generation got it right and chose forgiveness. Adding to the positive outcome, the younger generation watched and many years later chose forgiveness as well. Those that observe us may not remember our lectures or what we say, but will remember who we were and what they saw us do.

It's best when the older generation sets an example by making important decisions regarding relationships, property, and planning while they're able to do so. Someday the next generation may be dealing with similar issues. What we do or don't do matters and the impact may last for a long time.

Avoidable Regrets

In my view, "getting it right" with estate planning does not necessarily imply precision, but does imply an absolute best effort. Those affected by the plan may not agree with every provision. Nevertheless, knowing that a thorough process was followed in order to create the details and understanding why it was created as it was will help.

Time would likely prove that not giving this best effort would be an unacceptable regret. The relationship dangers that can arise due to improper planning, or no planning, can be significant. Litigation around probate issues can be costly and time-consuming. Wounded relationships may never be healed. Most would consider this type of damage to be an unacceptable regret.

From an estate planning standpoint, dividing up liquid cash among surviving family members is relatively simple. It just requires a calculator and a checkbook. However, for wealthy individuals it's usually more complicated. The list of assets may include ownership of a closely held business, a special personal residence, or other somewhat unique properties. Some of these assets may be what we might call legacy assets whereby there is a strong desire for the property to remain in the family.

It seems logical to allow adult siblings to own some of these legacy assets jointly, but sometimes that just doesn't work. For example, there may be a second family home involved where all the children spent a lot of time as they were growing up and many great family memories were created there.

If there are two or three siblings involved, there is a good chance that at least one of them won't be strongly attached to the property for whatever reason—the location may not be convenient; they may have a second home of their own; their spouse may hate the beach and prefer to spend time in the mountains—or it may be simple economics whereby one of the siblings can't afford their share of the maintenance expenses. Leaving this degree of complexity to be sorted out by heirs would likely prove to be an unacceptable regret.

The last time Melissa and I amended our personal plans, I made the comment to our attorney that since I can't see the future, there are aspects about the plan that give me pause. Our attorney quickly stated that yes, that's understandable, but we have to do the best we can with what we can see, and understand that we can change most of it later if we so desire. That's good advice.

Everyone involved knows that we did our best to get it right, why we did it, and in the end, that's all we can do. Regrets that would be simply unacceptable can usually be avoided, but a strategy is required.

PART II

TEN STRATEGIES TO AVOID REGRETS

CAREFULLY SELECT THE ADVISORY PLANNING TEAM

"It's unwise to pay too much, but it's unwise to pay too little. When you pay too much you lose a little money— that is all. When you pay too little, you sometimes lose everything because the thing you bought is incapable of doing the things you bought it to do. The common law of business practice prohibits paying a little and getting a lot. It can't be done. If you deal with the lowest bidder, it's well to add something for the risk you run. And if you do that, you will have enough to pay for something better."

– John Ruskin

The Planning Pattern

Generally, many high net worth individuals seem to be like the person in the circus who's in the midst of lots of poles with plates spinning at the top. They're running from pole to pole to keep the plates spinning so they will not fall off and break. What they would really like to have is help with the complexity of their lives and more time. They are risk takers, but there are aspects of their lives that they really would like to delegate.

From a financial standpoint, maybe their growth and complexity has grown slowly over time. Along the way, a collection of bank accounts, brokerage accounts, insurance policies, legal documents, entities, and relationships has evolved.

From a personal standpoint, maybe they now have a blended family or maybe a special needs child. At the very least, there are people in their lives with different dreams and challenges. They care about the uniqueness of the people in their lives but don't know how to help. They've heard about the concept of family governance and communication but really don't know where to start. They have worked hard over the years to create financial resources for themselves and their family, but now they realize it may be that the family is not really prepared for the money. In the middle of all of this, they really do not want to leave a mess for those who follow.

Hopefully a decision is made to reach out and be open to the development of a coordinated team of advisors. From a planning standpoint, I've noticed that there are four life stages that seem to motivate people to plan.

The first is when they are young and just starting out and maybe have few possessions, but have the desire to prepare for unforeseen events.

The second is usually around the time the first child is born. Young parents feel the need to have some life insurance and documents in place. It may be that the toughest decision they have to make is who will be the guardian of their child if both parents die. Sometimes this is easy and sometimes it's difficult.

The third time they may be motivated to plan is around the time they see their first grandchild. By now, their assets have grown and they're starting to realize that they may not live forever. Therefore, this round of planning may involve a more serious look at possible outcomes. It may be that there are in-laws in the picture now and decisions have to be made about the distribution of assets. In many cases it's helpful to create a diagram of how the estate assets will be distributed and the possible results.

Key decisions at this stage might be when to allow adult children access to the funds if both parents die. Conversations take place around the ability of various family members to manage money and whether or not some sort of protective device, such as a trust, should be considered to protect the assets and keep them in the family bloodline. Another unlikely but possible scenario has to be considered and that is what happens if the entire family dies in some sort of common catastrophe. Where should the money go if this happens?

The last time planning occurs is usually later in life and the objective is to make sure everything is buttoned-up and in order.

Because of the complexity of some of the decisions required at any of these points, procrastination is a risk. The motivational factor for getting it done might be a flowchart depiction of the current plan. A carefully selected planning team of advisors can help with this.

Trusted Advisors

Based upon my experiences, I'm a proponent of our clients having a carefully selected planning team. The team will be coordinated and at a minimum will consist of an estate planning attorney, a certified public accountant, a life insurance advisor, and a wealth manager. Ideally, the process works best if they all know each other and even better if from time to time the entire team meets together with the client.

I've noticed some value adding qualities over the years that the most successful advisors possess, such as:

1. They listen and take a personal interest in you, your family, and your concerns. Their agenda is not important and they're not just task and transaction oriented. They are concerned about your long-term goals and want to work with you to get it right. If you have a business, they will ask for a tour and want to understand what you do and how you do it. This will broaden their insight related to you and your business and enable them to know what questions to ask you. The more they know, the more helpful they can be.

2. They work well with your entire team of advisors. They will run ideas by the other team members in advance of presenting them to you so everyone will be in the loop and informed. With the team, there may be differences of opinions and approaches at times, which is not necessarily a bad thing. They're willing to defer to others, inside or outside their own firm, who may have greater expertise in a particular area. With a strong team of advisors, there will be respect for each

other's opinions, and information will be presented in a way that makes the choices clearer to you.

3. They will be a student of their area of specialty. Maintaining their technical edge will be a priority for them and they will be driven to be the "best in his or her class" at what they do professionally. They will not be a generalist.

4. They are good communicators and have the ability to help you consider the choices offered in a way that gives you confidence. Clarity will exist.

5. For their specialized practice, they will have a process to communicate trends in their area of specialty. Ours is a fast-changing world and the speed of change is accelerating. Planning will be a continuing process.

The development of a team often begins because the client has an established trust relationship with one of the advisors. That advisor then brings in additional members from his or her network that has been developed over the years as a result of working together. In most areas, the financial advisory community is a relatively close-knit group who value professional competence and integrity.

As with most groups, it's common for someone to informally serve in the "quarterback" role and be most aware of the client's ongoing agenda. As the life insurance advisor, I've found myself in that role frequently and am most happy to serve in this capacity. On the other hand, if I'm brought into the relationship by another advisor, I'm quite happy to serve with another team member being the de facto leader.

Most of our clients have relationships with the entire array of advisor categories noted above, but they would rarely be considered a team. Often we find that our client has outgrown some of their team members and needs to move on, even though it may involve the disengagement of a long relationship.

Detriments to the creation of an effective team include:

- A tendency to rely too heavily upon the opinion of family and friends

- Ties to a relationship that has been outgrown and the reluctance to get a second opinion

- A failure to recognize that a complex project requires outside experts

- An unrealistic view of the time commitment involved to get the process right

It may sound odd, but it's also advantageous to have advisors who are, when appropriate, willing to disagree with you and give the reasons for their position.

Information Overload

Technology is a wonderful tool and most of us use it every day—a lot. Access to information is easy and can be overwhelming. Recently due to over exercise, I think, I was experiencing pain in one of my knees so I Googled "knee pain" and received 28 million hits. After looking at some of the possibilities, I determined that the best thing for me to do was to seek the opinion of a qualified orthopedist.

A similar search turned up 200 million hits for estate planning, 465 million hits for life insurance, 158 million hits for power of attorney, and 2 million hits for irrevocable trusts. The confusion about which direction to pursue is not the result of too little information. We just a have a hard time knowing what to do with it. I submit that confusion and sometimes paralysis related to decisions is the result of information overload.

At the end of the day, most of us want a knowledgeable professional to listen and understand us. Then, afterward make an informed recommendation and clearly present the options, and better yet, care about the long-term end result.

Our clients understand leverage, that is, expanding some known facts beyond what is known in order to better understand aspects that are not so clear. As the issues and complexity grow, it becomes impractical to research and understand the details, so the need for delegation and a team results.

Since one individual can't possibly know everything about everything, specialization makes sense. If cancer develops, there's a need to see an oncologist. If a hip replacement is needed, there's a need to find a specialized orthopedist. While we might like to use our family practitioner for all of our needs, specialists are usually included in the conversation when complexity develops.

Seasoned advisors did not complete their education and immediately begin their career as an anointed and respected counselor. One of my favorite phrases is: "if you think education is expensive, you should try ignorance." Competence comes after years of acquiring technical knowledge, and along the way observing tools and techniques which work as well as others tried but proven to be ineffective. All of this is an ongoing process that never ends. Real-world experience honed by interactions with successful people with complicated issues is valuable. This happens one relationship at a time, the old-fashioned way.

Along the way, things happen that help advisors grow if they are able to survive. The process of surviving and working with different types of individuals with their own unique sets of challenges is an education that can add value to others. Being a high net worth individual or the owner of a closely held business can be lonely. The perspectives offered by the advisory team create confidence.

Most successful advisors are reliably on the client's side and sincerely want to help get it right for the family and avoid future regrets and surprises. The culture of the planning team makes a difference. The certified public accountant, estate planning attorney, insurance advisor, and wealth manager all have different and distinctive roles.

The Estate Planning Attorney

I've noticed that when people have estate planning on their mind there's an early need for a specialized estate planning attorney as a part of the advisory planning team. All of the different roles—the CPA and the tax issues, the attorney and the intricate planning and fine print legalese, the wealth manager, and the insurance advisor—have to all work together.

I've been involved in many sessions with clients as they review their objectives with the attorney and myself. Afterward, I've observed the end of the process where documents are about to be signed and heard the explanations of what the documents accomplish. Most feel really good once all the documents are signed because the plan is "cleaned up."

Clients are led through a process to help them think through their objectives and they are confident that the attorney understood what they said. It may have been that the attorney politely challenged some of their ideas, or they were gently corrected on some issues that could become problematic later on.

We live in a complicated world and as a result, it's best to choose individuals who are specialized according to what you need. For example, an attorney who is a litigator who helps clients protect themselves legally may not be the best person to create and design a complex estate plan. Similarly, the estate planning attorney is probably not the best person to go to court to protect a defendant.

It's my understanding that in recent years there's been an increase in self-prepared or "do-it-yourself" estate planning documents. In my view, this is not a good route to take. An attorney friend of mine shared with me that they were representing a bank that was involved with a complex estate that involved a self-prepared will for a decedent who had a second wife, adult children from a prior marriage, and several business interests. The costs in legal fees and delays in settling the estate were extreme.

A good estate planning attorney knows how to navigate a plan through complex estate and gift tax laws where they are applicable. They also know how to advise the client on "soft" issues, such as the equitable treatment of a current spouse and children by a previous marriage, how to provide for a child with special needs or other limitations, and the like.

Most people make an attempt to read the estate planning documents, but few are able to comprehend the legalese in the complicated strategies set forth in the documents in order to accomplish certain objectives. Therefore, making sure that the end objectives are clearly communicated and having confidence that the attorney understood and created the documents accordingly is of paramount importance.

Roles That Involve Responsibility

During the planning process, decisions will need to be made regarding the selection of an executor and most likely a trustee. The executor is responsible for locating and probating the decedent's will. This involves the collection of the decedent's property, the payment of debts, taxes, and expenses along with the distribution of any remaining assets to the beneficiaries specified in the decedent's will. An executor's responsibilities may last from one to five years.

A trustee is the person, or institution, named in a trust agreement to carry out the objectives and follow the terms of the trust. It's not unusual for the trustee's responsibilities to last for at least one generation and sometimes multiple generations. The trustee is responsible for investing the trust assets appropriately and prudently, as well as overseeing provisions for beneficiaries and upholding the specifics of the trust agreement.

The executor and trustee roles can be time-consuming and involve the risk of missing the mark and being challenged because of subpar attention or performance. For these reasons, often an institutional fiduciary is considered to serve in some capacity, perhaps as a co-trustee. Professional help is particularly important considering the ongoing and possibly very long-term responsibility related to being a trustee.

Most estate planning attorneys will, in addition to the will and any trust documents that might be required, also create power of attorney documents as well as health care directives. Managing a disabled relative's financial affairs with a power of attorney is complicated, but without the power of attorney, the complexity ramps up significantly. Without a financial power of attorney, a family member will likely have to go to court to be appointed as conservator or guardian of the property of their loved one. This can be expensive, in terms of legal fees and court costs. And, typically, it requires ongoing reports to the court throughout the time that the person is incapacitated.

The health care directive expresses the individual's desires related to end-of-life issues such as the use of feeding tubes and other means of prolonging life after there's no hope of recovery. In addition to the obvious reason for the document, it helps the family member think through and give the necessary instructions to the medical professionals because they will know what their parent or other family member wanted, as stated in the document. This process is often called for during times of emotional stress.

Five Ways the Estate Planning Attorney Can Provide Value

1. Your attorney brings specialized experience and knowledge. The documents that are created are all about you and your objectives for your family. Several documents may be involved, such as a will, power of

attorney, health care directive, irrevocable trust, revocable trust, and documents related to the continuation of a business, among others. This is a specialized process and all of the different pieces need to work together.

2. Your attorney is a careful listener. He or she helps you explore the nuances of your particular situation and perhaps identify concerns and solutions so that future misunderstandings and unintended consequences can be avoided. Future litigation may occur if vague language is included. Heirs may protest, saying, "Surely our parents didn't mean for this to happen this way." They may ask, "What's meant by equal treatment?" Two co-executors might be deadlocked regarding a decision with no provision to break the tie. The fine print matters.

3. Your attorney is an educator. The concepts and alternatives in estate planning are many and complex. The ability to explain complex solutions in understandable terms is valuable. It's customary to create a short summary related to each planning document. The summary does not replace the actual legal documents but serves as a narrative "road map" in understandable terms as to what the documents accomplish. Clients sometimes change the documents after they read the summary explanation. The summary will also likely be helpful to those who will be assisting later with the estate distributions, tax returns, and administration.

4. Your attorney will be efficient. Long lapses of time between conversations make the process cumbersome

because memories fade. Furthermore, with such important decisions being made, delay with the review and execution of the documents involves risk.

5. Your attorney is a team player and does not work in a silo. Of all your advisors, you probably spend the least amount of time each year with your attorney, but he or she remains in the loop. Their unique ability may not be that of a quarterback or a custodian of tax records — if not, that's okay. They advise and draft documents to match the objectives of the client keeping in mind the applicable state and federal laws.

The Certified Public Accountant (CPA)

As of this writing, income taxes on the wealthy have been increased, and there's not much reason to believe that sympathy for the wealthy will increase anytime soon. Because of this, most of our clients are looking for any and every legal way to reduce their tax bill. They also want to be aware of creative business succession techniques along with other strategies that address the client's concerns.

It's important for the CPAs to be in the mix because they are usually a confidant and quite familiar with the client and bring valuable experience. They have seen a lot because of their interactions with other similar clients and have a feel for what planning techniques work best. The relationship goes far beyond completing the annual income tax return.

For business owners, saving money on a tax-favored basis to supplement the limited 401(k) contributions is of interest. The CPA is familiar with available tax credits that might be important as well as more sophisticated tax and business planning opportunities like captive insurance companies and supplemental retirement plans. Their experience will be valuable in determining which are applicable and which are not. Even with the current estate tax exemptions, they will be familiar with gifting strategies and generation-skipping opportunities. A trusted CPA advisor brings a lot to the table.

Five Ways the CPA Can Provide Value

1. Your CPA should be as concerned with planning for next year's tax liabilities as they are with preparing your returns for the prior year. Often, upcoming tax liabilities can be reduced or mitigated by the use of appropriate tax planning strategies. Creative planning usually trumps just being a historian. It's a continuous engagement.

2. Your CPA can be a resource to provide creative planning ideas along with the ramifications involved. Proper planning will reduce tax cost, and planning will help the client present his financial statements in the most advantageous manner. Your CPA can be an advocate when securing financing or during the negotiation of a contract. Beyond tax advice, they can analyze the taxation outcomes of certain business decisions in order to help with decision-making. Your CPA will help you fully understand the risks and rewards of tax positions, which must be reasonable.

3. Your CPA should ask about and develop an under-standing related to the various members of your family

and extended family, which would include children, grandchildren, parents, and possibly others. An awareness of their general financial situations and your concerns about them can lead to planning suggestions that result in an overall decrease in the income, estate, and gift tax obligations of the family.

4. If you own a business, your CPA should be asking about your long-term plans for it. Is it your desire that it be or become a family or legacy business that survives in your family after you are not involved? Alternatively, is it a business that you intend to grow in a way that increases in value so that you can eventually monetize it through a sale or other exit strategy? Strategic decisions for the business can be very different depending on your intended destination.

5. Your CPA should be asking about, and aware of, the overall estate tax implications of the decisions you make. A clear understanding of your goals and values with respect to your family members, as well as your philanthropic interests, will influence recommendations and creative planning ideas. This brings greater value to you and your family.

The Life Insurance Advisor

Life insurance is a tax-advantaged asset that creates a cash death benefit. Currently, it can be arranged so that the cash arrives free of federal income, gift or estate tax, subject to exclusion amounts. From an estate planning standpoint, life insurance can be used to provide security for survivors, equalize the inheritance among heirs, cash for the payment of estate taxes, cash to fund a business succession plan, along with multiple other possibilities.

I've been a part of the life insurance advisor community since 1975, and I've seen several cycles related to life insurance products. Cycles have been caused by fluctuations with interest rates and investment returns that impact the performance of some of the products. Some products are designed with strong policy guarantees where the insurance company takes the risk. Other products are designed with a significant degree of flexibility that requires the policy owner to be engaged with the management of the policy.

Life insurance products are different from other financial assets in that health underwriting and approval are necessary in order to increase coverage or change from one provider to another. For example, premiums for the flexible policies that require management are based upon assumptions related to investment returns, cost of insurance, and other factors. If the assumptions are not met, additional premiums may be required in order to prevent the policy from lapsing. Life insurance surprises later in life are rarely pleasant because remedies may be limited.

Life insurance advisors, who are focused upon business owner and high net worth clients, typically operate as independent entrepreneurs. They represent the client and not a specific insurance carrier.

The role of the insurance advisor is to listen to the client, help identify the financial concerns, and then create options that fit the need. Key factors are the health status of the client, the ability to pay premiums, the amount of coverage that's necessary, and how long it needs to last.

In addition, the structure related to ownership and beneficiary designations is important. Based upon our experience over the years, we recommend a conservative approach to life insurance. Assuming that the coverage will not be needed after ten or fifteen years may prove to be shortsighted.

Personally, if I was a prospective client myself, I would want to see options from various financially sound insurance companies. Each company will have already considered and made a tentative decision on the final rates that I might be offered based upon my circumstances. The underwriting process that determines the actual rates is a competitive process within itself.

I would also like to know about possible surprises that may happen down the road and have an understanding as to how the future relationship would be managed.

Five Ways the Life Insurance Advisor Can Provide Value

1. Your life insurance advisor is a problem solver and has a process that is focused upon you and not a product. Products available today are complex and the spectrum from conservative to aggressive covers a wide span. An important advisor role is to understand the client's comfort level with risk so that the options can be developed and understood.

2. Your life insurance advisor is a good listener and helps you define your objectives. The analysis of the insurance

needed both now and in the future will require facts related to current assets, your concerns about dangers that may be present in the future, as well as some assumptions related to the future.

3. Your life insurance advisor has direct access to multiple financially sound insurance companies. Insurance companies attempt to differentiate themselves with the various products they offer. One company may have a focus upon products that accumulate cash while another may be focused on providing a guaranteed death benefit that lasts long into the future. Objectivity along with the desire to represent the client's best interest is valuable.

4. Your life insurance advisor has a defined process for needs analysis, product selection, and the underwriting process. A defined process ensures that all clients have the opportunity for the same experience, but tailored to their own circumstances. The underwriting process is a differentiator. Allowing multiple insurance companies to compete among themselves with regard to their underwriting offer can make a significant difference to the client.

5. Your life insurance advisor views the client as a relationship as opposed to viewing the policy acquisition as a transaction. An extended team is in place to handle the ongoing review, service, and relationship that may extend over several decades. Life insurance products require ongoing management.

The Wealth Manager

Many of our clients have the bulk of their assets in illiquid properties such as closely held businesses or real estate. But, for those who have had a liquidity event such as a sale of a business or property, or maybe even a distribution from a retirement plan, they will likely want and need help managing the money.

I have delivered life insurance claim checks to beneficiaries who really did not know what to do with the cash. That said, the wealth management business is somewhat segregated by the amount of assets available to be invested. For example, some well-known firms have a minimum of $100 million; others have a $25 million minimum or a $2 million minimum and so forth. Others have lower minimums, but my point is that whatever cash you have to invest is very important to you and finding an appropriate advisor that's a good fit, makes sense.

Many members of the World War II generation retired with defined benefit plans. This means a check for a certain amount was delivered each month. Some of their children have ended up with defined benefit plans too. But, many have been transitioned to defined contribution plans such as 401(k) plans. Under these plans, they will largely control their own destiny depending on how much they decide to invest as well as how effectively they invest the money.

Similarly, those who have sold a business or created cash in some other way may be financially dependent upon their nest egg. The prospect of thirty, and possibly more, years of retirement coupled with the uncertainty of future events requires diligence with regard to how available funds are invested.

Our economy is complex and increasingly affected by international events and governmental actions. A relationship with a wealth management advisor, an important member of your advisory planning team, can create an added amount of comfort and support.

Five Ways the Wealth Manager Can Provide Value

1. Your wealth manager has a depth of resources that includes a process to manage all of your financial assets oriented such that you will not outgrow their capabilities. In addition, they are knowledgeable and helpful with regard to wealth and estate planning and possibly even banking as well.

2. Your manager will likely prefer to consolidate all of your accounts onto one platform. However, there may be some assets that you prefer to keep separate due to previous relationships or other considerations, but the manager should have the ability to recognize these outside assets. This will ensure that proper asset allocation and diversification strategies be managed based upon your tolerance for risk. In addition, the overlap of holdings in various accounts can be monitored.

3. Your wealth manager coordinates the tax implications and administrative costs of your investments with your CPA and communicates these costs to you. A full disclosure of fees will be provided. Attention given to creating a plan that is efficient from a tax standpoint can add to the effective return on the assets.

4. Your wealth manager will want to know you and the other important people in your life. Furthermore, there may be certain industries in which you do not want to invest. They will want to know your other advisors and receive clear direction from you as to whom they may speak with regarding your financial affairs. Clear direction regarding who may direct investment decisions will be obtained.

5. Your wealth manager will be oriented toward comprehensive planning along with ongoing review and service. The process will include the creation of a written investment policy statement based upon a careful understanding of your objectives. Your money is being managed for a reason. It may be that you are planning to start a business. Or, you may be planning to retire. Your objectives need to be identified. It may be that financial projections need to be made in order to make sure there's enough money to retire. This is particularly important if a business is being sold. It's important that the "final paycheck," considering taxation, is enough to provide a secure future.

Bringing It All into Focus

Over the years, I've had many eye exams and noticed that there is a process for both eyes involved with the evaluation. At the end, there's a moment when everything comes together, and the chart on the wall is in focus.

Similarly, from time to time it's advisable, with the help of the advisory team, to pretend that death has occurred. The first step is to provide a complete financial statement that includes how the various assets are owned and titled. Also include all retirement plans and life insurance in effect indicating the ownership and beneficiary designations.

The second step is to develop a flowchart that details when, where, and how the various assets flow according to the legal documents in place and the provisions that are included.

A Word about the Team Selection Process

Most advisors have an introductory process that involves no fee or commitment from the prospective new client. For the wealth management advisor, this might include a risk audit of the prospect's current investment portfolio to determine asset classes and possibly fees that are involved.

For the attorney and CPA advisor role, the introductory conversation most likely would include listening to the prospect's objectives and getting some preliminary observations followed by a recommendation and a proposed fee. The listening process may involve more than one visit because this is a critical phase. The more the advisor understands about the client the better he or she is able to help.

For the insurance advisor role, the introductory phase may include a conversation about the objectives as well as a review of existing coverage. With proper authorization, the advisor can obtain current projections and facts related to existing coverage from the present insurance companies. Also, a process of obtaining some tentative underwriting offers from various insurance companies may be included. This involves the electronic submission, with the client's authorization, of medical records to various insurance carriers. This step is often necessary because it is unrealistic to ask for a commitment prior to knowing the facts and options.

Clarity, Direction, and Ongoing Help

After many years of interacting with clients, quite a few stories have developed. Recommendations are made based upon the facts that the advisors have to work with. Usually, the clients accept the recommendations, but sometimes they do not.

We have given a lot of thought to what the experience is like when an initial visit takes place to discuss our process for insurance and estate planning. Typically, the new client has been referred to us by one of their other advisors such as their attorney, accountant, or wealth manager. Therefore, there's a degree of trust that has been transferred already.

Our clients are usually busy people who are taking time to do something that they understand is important. They are talking to us because they want direction. Many times, it's unnatural to slow down and ask for direction. This is particularly true for type A personalities.

We understand how the process feels and have given some thought to what they might be thinking when we first meet. For some, it's uncomfortable to essentially say, "I'm here because there are people in my life that I love and I want to protect." Furthermore, some of the business owners and wealthy individuals with whom we work bring baggage from prior relationships with other past financial advisors.

They're also most likely thinking that the tools and techniques used for planning are complicated and not readily understood. Clients are asking for clarity and our help.

Often something has prompted them to initiate the conversation. It may have been the concern of one of their other advisors. It may be that a relative or friend has died and sometimes it may even be because they've received a concerning report from their physician. Maybe there's a sense of urgency because of an upcoming trip and they want to make sure that everything is in order. All in all, we do our best to make the experience easy because conceptually we know why they want to talk.

Having Structure in Place to Manage Complexity Is Wise

The creation of a functioning advisory team will increase the likelihood that what you want to happen will actually take place. During the process, you will have been challenged to think through and be specific about your objectives. The result will be that coordinated plans will be in place, and a team that knows you will be able to assist those left behind as the plan is carried out into the future.

Complexity and Confusion

As your estate is settled, life for your heirs continues. Having an advisory team in place who has listened to you and helped create your plan minimizes the possibility of later complexity, confusion, and costly surprises. Lack of clarity may be detrimental to future relationships among people you care about.

CREATE A PROCESS FOR ASSET TRANSITIONS

"There are risks and costs to a program of action, but they are far less than the long-range risks and costs of a comfortable inaction."

– John F. Kennedy

Creation and Hand Off of a Business:
Both Are a Challenge

Starting a business is usually difficult. Equally challenging is positioning the business so it can carry on when the entrepreneur is no longer around. Entrepreneurs begin with a dream for what the business might become, and in some ways, it resembles a child they created and raised. There are dreams for its growth and continuing future.

There are really three options waiting at some point down the road for a business owner. One option is successfully positioning the business in the hands of a new generation of owners that may be family or nonfamily.

A second option is to sell the business, take the cash, and either retire or begin something new.

A third and unattractive option is to allow the business to die a sudden or slow death where it gradually glides into the dirt due to lack of innovation, interest, or talent.

Transition and Survival

As an illustration of the importance of having a business succession plan in place and funded, let's review Jon and Sid's situation. I was introduced to Jon by his CPA. Jon and Sid were 50/50 owners of a construction company and they were also great friends. They had developed a niche whereby they constructed stand-alone retail buildings all over the southeast for a national organization.

As is often the case, they began their business together after leaving a larger company where they had become acquainted over the years. They realized their dream involved risk and knew, in the early years, the financial reward would be nominal.

As the business began to grow, it became something akin to a child they were raising together, and it became an important part of their self-worth and identity. Over time, the business began to take on a life of its own and its value as an ongoing enterprise grew.

Jon was single, and Sid had a wife and two children away at college. One morning, Jon called me and was crying. He told me that Sid had played tennis the night before, and just after he came home, he collapsed on the kitchen floor and died.

Only a couple of years before, Jon's CPA and I invited a mutual friend of ours who is an estate planning attorney to a meeting with Jon and Sid. We discussed the importance of having a business succession plan and Jon and Sid decided to proceed. A buy/sell agreement was created that provided for each to own three million dollars of life insurance on the other. An agreement was in place whereby the insurance proceeds, if a death occurred, would be used to purchase the deceased's ownership interest in the business from the estate.

In addition to the buy/sell arrangement, we also implemented a one million dollar life insurance policy on both Jon and Sid that was owned by and payable to the business.

After Sid's death, everything worked as planned. Jon personally received a check for three million dollars because he was the owner and the beneficiary of the policy on Sid. According to the agreement, Jon then purchased the 50 percent ownership interest in the business from Sid's estate.

The end result was that Jon received a three million dollar increase in his tax basis in the business because he purchased it personally. He now owned 100 percent of the firm. Sid's estate received three million dollars in cash, and because Sid's tax basis in the business stepped up to the value at the time of his death, there was no income tax due upon the sale of his business interest.

Without this arrangement and funding, Jon would have found himself in business with Mary, Sid's widow. When such situations happen, typically the widow or widower is an inactive owner but desires and needs income. Sometimes they wish to become an active owner, but may not possess the skills for this to work.

It's helpful to consider that Mary took great pride in the success of the business along with Sid. It became an integral part of both of their lives. Now the dynamics have changed. The transition away from the business requires a careful process because ownership frequently has emotional as well as financial repercussions.

Being in business with Mary would have put Jon in a tough spot because Mary was inexperienced and unable to really contribute to the business. On top of that, someone would have to be hired to fill Sid's role in the operation of the business. Knowing Jon as I do, he would not want to short Mary in any way, and he would be torn between being fair to Mary and keeping the business viable.

If the agreement and funding had not been in place, Jon could have agreed to purchase Mary's ownership interest, but that would have been a significant cash drain for a long time and inefficient from an income tax standpoint. John's payments to Mary to purchase the business over time would be made out of his after-tax income. On top of all of this, Jon still would need to either assume Sid's responsibilities in the business or hire a replacement. None of these choices would be good, so fortunately the plan was in place and it worked.

Survival of the Business

As noted above, the business also received life insurance proceeds of one million dollars income tax-free to compensate for the loss of a key person. The corporate business agreements specifically excluded these cash proceeds from the value of the business for buyout purposes. Had this provision not been in place, it's possible that the value of the business for buyout purposes would have been inflated by the life insurance proceeds. The estate then would essentially own 50 percent of the cash intended to help with the transition. That would have been an expensive surprise for Jon.

The key-person insurance was important because Jon and Sid both brought different and somewhat unique talents to the business and one would be significantly hampered without the other. Jon was more of an inside guy, and Sid was more of an outside guy, who managed projects and relationships. Furthermore, the business had a credit line which, because of their growth, was sometimes fully utilized creating stress for the owners.

Therefore, because of the buy/sell arrangement, it's good that Jon now owns 100 percent of the business and Mary has been cashed out. But he still has a business to run and lingering debts to pay, and he has lost Sid, the primary relationship manager with the firm's key client.

The one million dollar key person policy provided a transitional cushion, which has allowed the business to prosper and continue to grow. Jon was grateful that the plans were in place and that there were no surprises along the way. Cash is a great reliever of stress and has a soothing effect on the nerves in situations like these.

The Legal Documents Had Not Been Updated

Everything went smoothly from a business transition standpoint, but on the personal side, things were somewhat complicated. About ten years prior to his death, Sid and Mary had created new wills and established an irrevocable trust for estate planning purposes. The trust purchased insurance on Sid's life.

Unfortunately, the executor of Sid's estate was his older brother Frank, who had since moved to Chicago because of his employment. Frank was also the trustee for the trust. Because of Sid's death, the executor and trustee had important responsibilities to meet. The successor to Frank on both documents was Mary's father-in-law, who was now suffering from the early stages of dementia.

Because of the distance, logistics, and as it turned out less-than-ideal relationships, it was no longer best for Frank to serve as executor and trustee. Fortunately, the documents included provisions that allowed him to resign and appoint someone else more appropriate to serve the family.

The roles of the executor, as well as trustee, include important responsibilities that are at times more difficult than they would initially seem. Geographic proximity helps. Familiarity with the family helps. A younger age than the estate owner is a good thing. But, character is crucial. Aristotle defined character as a type of habit that's been shaped by choice into an active condition of choosing well.[1] This type of habit is a high standard that's usually formed over time and doesn't change overnight.

While we do not give legal or tax advice, we've seen the importance of a regular review of the estate planning legal documents. Sid's personal side of the story is an example of the importance of having a team of specialists who are allowed to become involved in both the business and the personal planning.

---

[1] Aristotle, *Nichomachian Ethics*, Book II, Chapters 1 and 5.

In Sid's case, he had a team of advisors for the business planning, but he kept his personal planning separate. It's best if all of the various pieces are coordinated.

A recommendation also had been made to Sid and Mary, but not acted upon, concerning the way some of their real estate holdings were titled and owned. The property that was owned jointly passed directly to Mary instead of flowing through the estate plan as created by the estate planning documents.

At the moment of death, the person is gone and the need for estate management arrives. Bank accounts are frozen and business cannot be done until the will is recorded and "letters testamentary" are issued. These "letters" are proof of the legal authority of the personal representative to collect and deal with the assets of the decedent's estate.

Most of us are mostly tranquil about the fact that we will someday die. We know that it will happen but spend very little time thinking about it.

Future Regrets That Were Avoided

- Mary's continued financial dependence upon the business

- Jon's tax inefficient and costly purchase of Sid's interest in the business from Mary

- Financial hardship on the business because of the loss of Sid's talents

- Mary's dependence upon a distant executor and trustee

Regrets That Could Have Been Avoided

- Complexity caused by Sid's lack of coordination of personal plans and business plans

- Complexity caused by the designated trustee being unable to effectively serve

Minority Ownership

Those who have seen business transitions occur and estates be probated and settled are inclined to be committed to paying attention to the details of their own plans. We learn a lot by settling the estate of a family member or living through the transition of a key business partner who leaves a business for whatever reason.

Many of our clients are closely held businesses, and "closely held" does not necessarily mean a small mom-and-pop business. As businesses grow over time, the ownership of the business may be spread over several owners. From a business and estate planning standpoint, the difference between being a minority owner and a controlling owner is significant. The laws of simple mathematics indicate that if a decision comes to a vote, 51 percent will always be greater than 49 percent and will win the vote.

We have seen arrangements that worked and some that didn't. My personal opinion is that 50/50 percent ownership between two individuals can work, but it's better if someone is in charge. If two 50/50 owners disagree, a stalemate can occur.

Along this line of thinking, consider what would happen if two 50/50 owners decide to give a key employee 10 percent ownership. It's logical to think they still control 90 percent of the vote. They do, but if the two of them disagree, the 10 percent owner can cast his vote one way or the other and control the outcome. The vote would be 55/45. That is power and a degree of control.

The 10 percent owner can be fired as an employee, but as long as he owns a portion of the business, he can vote and has certain legal access to the details related to the operation of the business.

Maintaining Control

It is possible for surprises to take place. Andrew owns the largest stake in a large closely held business that has nine shareholders. His ownership, coupled with that of his two adult children who work in the business, constitutes a majority ownership of the outstanding stock.

I was asked to review a life insurance policy on Andrew and learned, to everyone's surprise, that the premium was about to escalate dramatically. The policy was owned by and payable to the business, and an agreement was in place requiring the business to purchase Andrew's stock in the event of his death. From a simplicity standpoint, this seemed appropriate.

The cash for the purchase of Andrew's stock would be created by the life insurance policy, so it was important to structure the insurance coverage so that it would remain in place permanently. Andrew's health was good, even though he was approaching seventy years old, so the transition from one policy to a new one with significant premium guarantees was relatively simple.

But, if Andrew's stock was purchased upon his death by the business, the result would be fewer outstanding shares owned by the remaining shareholders. This would cause the ownership percentages to shift among the remaining owners. Sometimes this can have unintended consequences. The math, after the ownership percentages shift, will determine who or what group possesses voting control of the business.

Andrew's objective is for his two children to continue control of the business after he is no longer involved. However, upon review, it was determined that if Andrew's stock is purchased by the business, and later one of his children dies and their stock is also purchased by the business, the remaining child would be in a minority stock ownership position. This would be an unintended consequence of the plan.

We developed a chart that illustrated different scenarios, remote as they may seem, whereby voting control of the business could shift away from the family and into the hands of older, inactive individuals. In business, as in most of life, it's preferable to avoid negative surprises.

The solution was to implement a cross purchase buy/sell agreement whereby the family members agreed to purchase the shares if another family member died. This way the shares stay in the family. Otherwise, shares purchased by the business are diluted among all the owners, which could shift ownership control away from the family.

Future Regrets That Were Avoided

- Dramatic life insurance premium increase
- Loss of family control

GENERATIONAL IMPACT

Surprises during a Transitional Period Can Be Negative

It's a safe assumption that owners of businesses will someday leave the business, one way or the other. When a death occurs, those left in the business can include family members as well as nonfamily members. Since the business is frequently a substantial financial contributor to the security of those who survive, it is prudent to have well constructed plans—business and personal—in place.

AVOIDABLE REGRET

Disruption and Unexpected Cost

Inserting an uninvolved owner/surviving spouse suddenly onto the board or management team of a closely held business is a challenge for both the business and the surviving spouse. Under these circumstances, realizing the full value of the deceased owner's interest is difficult and can impact the future financial security of the survivors. This is in addition to the awkwardness and potential damage to the relationships both inside and outside of the business.

PLAN FOR FLEXIBILITY

"If you don't like change, you're going to like
irrelevance even less."

– Gen. Eric Shinseki, US Army Chief of Staff

Life Insurance Is an Asset

I've been in the life insurance business for almost forty years and I've seen that while the coverage, an asset, remains in place, the need and the purpose for the coverage often changes over time. People change, the economy changes, tax laws change, and come to think of it, most things in life can change. Therefore, plans and tools utilized evolve over time. Therefore, flexibility is valuable.

One example of evolving needs that illustrate the value of flexibility is with the family of David and Alice. Two of the four adult children of David and Alice came by my office to review a last-to-die life insurance policy that was implemented on their parents many years ago. The two oldest children are the co-trustees of the irrevocable trust that owns the policy. At the time the coverage was initiated, its purpose was to provide cash for estate taxes that would be due largely because of a legacy piece of property they wanted to remain in the family.

Because of changes with the estate tax laws, the tax is no longer a present concern to them. But, family financial reversals had caused them to view the life insurance policy as a conservative investment that would create a tax free cash death benefit now needed to fund new needs that have developed.

The cash would be used to equalize the inheritance among their four children. As the years passed, it became clear that only one of the four children had an interest in the family's lake home. Careers had taken two of the children to other parts of the country and the remaining child preferred a place at the beach instead of a shared lake home. The life insurance asset that will create cash when the last parent dies will allow the lake home to pass to the one child that wants it. The other three children will receive an amount of cash so that all four children receive equal value.

Another factor that emerged with the passage of time was the arrival of nine grandchildren along with their educational needs. Furthermore, one of the grandchildren has special needs.

All four of the adult children realized from the beginning that the ultimate death benefit from this policy would not benefit their parents because it is a policy designed to create cash upon the last survivor's death.

The decision was made to appoint two of the four children to assume the responsibility of being co-trustees. The parents, David and Alice, funded the trust checking account with cash gifts around Christmas time each year, which was well before the annual premiums were due. The co-trustees were meticulous and kept careful records and provided the trust beneficiaries with the proper notices related to the gifts, as instructed by their estate planning attorney.

We sometimes see the original need for life insurance go away only to be replaced by a new need that was not present earlier. Someday the cash that will be created by this insurance policy will accomplish new objectives that have emerged for this extended family. This is an example of why it's important to plan, be flexible, and take the conservative approach.

It may be true that they don't actually need life insurance for the traditional reasons of supporting a surviving family, and they may not need it for estate tax. But, if they have maintained the policy over the years, discontinuing it just as life expectancy approaches may be costly to the surviving family. Based on my experience, a need will likely be present and if not, an opportunity to help a charitable cause may provide a lot of satisfaction.

Trying to predict the future is dicey at best because the speed of change is accelerating. One of my all-time favorite movies, *Father of the Bride*, has a line that I like. The wedding planner is reviewing the cost of the wedding with the overwhelmed father of the bride and states, "Welcome to the nineties, Mr. Banks." Family trends are changing and it seems that constant adaptation is the norm. Adult children may not move out until they become married, and when they do move out, they may move far away. Older family members may move in with children in their later years. All of this is hard to predict years in advance.

A prevalent fear is that of growing old, possibly being alone, and wondering about the expense and discomfort of the later years. The prevalence of dementia has been growing, and spending a few years in an assisted living facility can be expensive. It may be that maintaining a life insurance policy until it matures as a death claim could make sense for the family in order to reimburse the estate for the expense of the final years. We've seen this happen many times.

Life insurance is an asset that, if properly managed and structured, will ultimately create capital if held to maturity. The reasons for maintaining the coverage will likely change over the years.

Future Regrets That Were Avoided

- The sale of the lake home in order to equalize the inheritance among the heirs

- Long-term financial stresses on adult children caused by the expenses related to grandchildren

Capital Creation

Another example of evolving needs and the value of flexibility was with Bob and Nell. They were farmers in south Georgia. I met them through a banker in their hometown. During the 1990s, many community banks began marketing financial products such as life insurance and annuities. I was approached by an organization that provided "back office" services to community banks and asked to partner with them, as needed, and be the out-of-town life insurance and estate planning expert for the bank's high net worth customers.

The strategy included me being a speaker at business oriented social events organized by the banks. I think the longest day of my career occurred during this time. I left my home near Atlanta around five a.m. and was the guest speaker at a breakfast organized by a bank in middle Georgia, a couple of hours away. After the breakfast, I drove south and was a speaker at a luncheon meeting at a bank near Waycross in south Georgia. After that, I drove over to the Georgia coast to a bank near Brunswick for a dinner meeting. I then drove back to Atlanta and arrived home sometime after midnight.

We learned that most of the people that came to the bank organized events were not good prospects for what we were doing. Our best prospects seemed to decline the broad invitations and were best met through a personal introduction by the local bank president. This is how I met Bob and Nell.

At the time I was introduced to them, they had three large life insurance policies that had not been reviewed for several years. Because of the bank president's introduction and their relationship with him, they trusted me immediately. Trust has to be earned over a long period of time but can be "jump started" by the endorsement of a mutual friend.

I am gratified by relationships of this type, but I was a little uncomfortable with their first request. I needed access to the existing life insurance policies in order to initiate a review. Since my family and I were planning to be on our way to Florida on a Sunday a few days after our initial visit, I suggested that I stop by and pick up the policies. Bob said that they would be away at church so I should just stop by their place and the policies would be on the kitchen table. The back door would be unlocked. Going by their unoccupied home on a Sunday morning made me uncomfortable, but at the same time it was refreshing.

With their signed authorization, I was able to contact their existing insurance carriers and obtain all of the facts, figures, and projections that we needed in order to fully understand the contracts. As it turned out, the life insurance policies they had were underperforming and the coverage likely would not last until Bob's death without increased premiums.

The insurance policies were also owned by Bob personally which meant that the death proceeds could ultimately be subject to estate tax. Bob was aware of this and generally familiar with some of the techniques used to protect insurance proceeds from tax. But, he had procrastinated because of the horror that he had watched unfold within his older brother's family.

Bob's brother passed away when he was in his early fifties, and about ten years later the brother's wife passed away. Much of the family farm and business was left in trust for the surviving siblings. I was not privy to the details, but Bob shared with me that the siblings disagreed with each other on the direction of the business. They also disagreed with positions taken and the amount of control exercised by the trustee. Lawsuits were involved. According to Bob, the trustee was a friend of his brother but simply not equipped to handle the complexity of the family and business dynamics. The standard of behavior required for trustees is high. It can be a demanding role.

Observing his brother's family disagreements made Bob and Nell reluctant to make decisions because they lacked confidence. After our initial conversations, I introduced Bob and Nell to a new estate planning attorney and CPA. They had simply outgrown their previous relationships. The team developed a plan that involved a trust that would protect the life insurance from estate taxes and facilitate the distribution ultimately to their heirs. Additional trusts were involved with the estate plan as well. Because of the complexity, liability, and possible longevity of the trusts, Bob and Nell made the decision to select a corporate trustee.

Many years ago, it was considered almost unethical to replace an existing life insurance policy. The industry has changed and new generations of policies are now available. A financial analysis of available options compared to the facts obtained related to the present insurance will determine whether the policy should be kept or replaced. Obviously, any new coverage will involve an assessment of ongoing health issues and health history. Because of Bob's good health at the time, we exchanged the policies for newer and better coverage after reviewing the alternatives.

Often the transition from an old policy to a new one is accomplished by a process structured as a 1035 tax-free exchange. Under this arrangement, any taxable gain in the old policy is not recognized as it is transferred into the new policy. The cash surrender value that is transferred into the new policy can buy down the future premium outlay projected for the new policy.

For Bob and Nell, the years passed by and debts were incurred to support the farming operation, and other unexpected financial reversals occurred as well. We had conversations about the difficulty of continued and somewhat large gifts to the trust. Fortunately, because the new policies were relatively flexible, we used some of the accumulated cash to keep them in effect.

Bob died when he was in his late eighties. He had become frail and his major organs were beginning to fail. Up until the final months of his life, he still insisted on driving the tractor every day—much to the chagrin of Nell. That's just the way he was. During his last hospital stay, Nell was called to the hospital one morning around two in the morning. She was told that Bob was experiencing kidney failure. She was asked about her opinion regarding next steps, which included the possibility of heroics. Because the planning team had thoroughly discussed the health care directive and heard Bob express his feelings, Nell sadly let him go. The health care directive—sometimes called a living will—has value from a legal standpoint as well as from an emotional standpoint for those who must make decisions.

Shortly thereafter, I drove down to deliver the life insurance proceeds to the trustee and Nell. I've learned from experience that delivering life insurance claim checks can be an emotional experience for the beneficiary, and almost always an emotional experience for me. We sat in her kitchen and talked for a while, and as the time neared for me to leave we were standing next to the kitchen table. I pulled the envelope that contained the check out of my coat pocket. As I held the envelope toward the trustee, Nell hugged me.

To her, the check represented a degree of financial provision from Bob, for her, and the entire family. The cash would eliminate their debts and cure most of the financial problems that had plagued them in recent years. That's exactly what Bob wanted to happen.

The original purpose of the insurance changed from being purely an estate tax solution, and now included provision for debt repayment even later in life, which years ago was not expected.

In my world, this is an example of what it means to have flexible plans that financially protect the family, and why they're important.

The Soft Side of the Plan—the Non-Financial Assets

Over the years, I had gotten to know and work with Bob and Nell's extended family that included a son and a daughter, along with their in-laws and six grandchildren. The son, daughter, and son-in-law all worked in the family farming business, which because of the transition planning and life insurance funding, would be able to continue after Bob and Nell's death.

About five years after Bob's death, Nell died after a short bout with cancer. All aspects of the plan worked as intended. Largely due to the encouragement of the estate planning attorney, Bob and Nell had carefully planned for the transfer of their personal non-financial assets to the next two generations.

As is the case with most family homes, included were objects that everyone might want that aren't divisible. Often, the legal estate plan leaves personal objects to the surviving spouse and then to their children to divide. How this process ultimately goes can have an impact on the relationships among the extended family going forward. Usually it is not so much the financial value of the property, but the sentimental value that's important to an heir.

Bob and Nell had lived a long and prosperous life and had accumulated items as they traveled and inherited some objects from their ancestors. For example, Bob's father had found a Civil War cannonball somewhere north of Atlanta, and it had been in Bob's room as he grew up and remained in their home until his death. Nell's mother had passed along a pie safe that had been in her family's home as she grew up. Their home included artwork and pottery from around the world that they had purchased on their travels. Included was a pottery vase that they purchased in Tuscany, artistic plates from Lisbon, Portugal, and glasswork from Murano near Venice, Italy.

Bob and Nell decided to walk around their home with their son and daughter, long before either of them became sick, and retold the stories related to these one-of-a-kind objects. Decisions were made along the way as to who would get what, and a letter of instruction was written and filed with their other important papers. Leaving the children to figure all this out later would have entailed relationship risk.

Future Regrets That Were Avoided

- Allowing life insurance policies to lapse prior to death

- Being forced to work with an unacceptable trustee

- Financial stress during the last years of Nell's life because of illiquid property and ongoing debt

- Possible family discord caused by the claiming of personal property

GENERATIONAL IMPACT

Planning for Change Is Wise

People and circumstances evolve as time passes. It may be that plans are initially created in order to provide family security. The need may evolve to include keeping together what the family has been able to put together along with multiple special needs. The uniqueness of the future set of facts is difficult to foresee. Flexibility has value.

AVOIDABLE REGRETS

Roadblocks and Rigid Alternatives

It is natural to become attached to our property that we have grown to love and enjoy. There is often a desire that these properties, financial and personal, remain in the family. Forced liquidation or contentious disbursement of property for any reason is unfortunate. Rigid, shortsighted plans can result in disappointment for us and those we care about.

FOCUS ON THE NEEDS OF OTHERS

"When a man does not know which harbor he is heading for, no wind is the right wind."

– Seneca

Yogi Berra's well-known comment, "It ain't over till it's over," is a great observation about sporting events ending when the clock runs out, but it's not an accurate statement about the impact of our lives.

Many years ago, I developed the habit of leaving sporting events a few minutes early. When our children were in elementary school, the college basketball games on school nights created a conflict with their bedtime routine. We often slipped out of games early to avoid the traffic and listened to the final minutes on the radio on the way home. Often there was a game changer at the very end, which we missed, but when the clock ran out the game was over and recorded.

When we die, yes, our lives are over; but in a way, everything around us continues. That is: our families, our debts, our businesses, and whatever plans we had in place continue on and have an impact.

A Thirty-Year Relationship

Ellen's story is one of the best illustrations of the generational echo and the resolve to protect loved ones that I've seen. I met Ellen through one of my friends early in my career. She worked long hours to build the small business that she owned. At the time she became a client, she did not have a relationship with an active insurance professional.

Besides being a client she also became a good friend, and as a side note, I recall a comment she made early on about making an investment in friends. Up until that time, I'd never thought about being intentional and investing time and resources in developing friendships. I thought they just happened. Looking back, conversations that I've had through the years with Ellen, and other wise individuals like her, have been valuable.

Over the years, we reviewed Ellen's needs for her family and her business and added various insurance policies along the way. One was a $300,000 term life insurance policy owned by a trust designed to provide funds to educate her children. During one of our conversations, Ellen said that she was thinking about discontinuing the gifts to the trust because her children were grown and educated. Besides, the premiums on the term policy were significant and rising because of her advancing age. Ellen's health was not good. She'd had two heart attacks, bypass surgery, and had almost died a couple of times.

Rather than simply allowing the term policy to lapse, we discussed the possibility of the trustee selling the policy to a third party. The market has softened somewhat in recent years, but at the time, there was a vibrant market for life insurance policies particularly where the insured was older and in poor health. As you would suspect, the interest in buying policies and the price willing to be paid rises as the health worsens.

We submitted her health history to several possible buyers and the best offer received was in excess of $60,000. And, this is for the policy that the trustee was planning to simply cancel. After presenting this possibility to the trustee, who happened to be Ellen's son, the comment was, "Wow, if the policy is worth that much to a stranger maybe we should keep it."

The trustee decided to convert the term policy to a permanent policy that had a level premium and was guaranteed for life as long as the premiums were paid. This conversion could be done without submitting medical history to the insurance company.

The next chapter of the story took place a few years later after Ellen's health had further declined and the economy was now taking a toll on her once prosperous business. Besides the trust-owned policy mentioned above, there were three additional policies in place on Ellen's life. From these policies, almost $300,000 of cash loans had been made.

Keeping the coverage in place was getting expensive because of the ongoing premiums. Plus, interest on the policy loans must be paid and the interest was not tax-deductible. Furthermore, the ongoing low interest-rate environment was hurting the performance of the policies.

Ellen never expected to have significant debt at this point in her life. Therefore, keeping the insurance in place, since Ellen was in her eighties, was important to the financial healing for her surviving family. She never expected to be in this position and was committed to seeing the program through.

After looking at all the options, the decision was made to obtain a $300,000 bank loan to repay the policy loans. The insurance policies were pledged as collateral for the bank loan. Now that the cash is back into the insurance policies they will perform better and require lower ongoing premiums. And, the interest on the bank loan is less than the interest that was being paid on the policy loans.

All in all, Ellen was sacrificing some cash flow in her later years that she never thought would be necessary. As a result, a death benefit would be created to provide security for her surviving spouse and succeeding generations. Making this provision was important to Ellen because her focus was upon the well-being of others after she was gone.

I've noticed that professional insurance advisors are usually most proficient with maintaining personal relationships. It is very rewarding to observe someone financially protecting others they love. We enjoy the development of relationships, but as a group, our track record is marginal with regard to transitioning those relationships to a successor, who will be able to maintain them after we are no longer active in the business. The transition requires time and a younger partner to assume the relationship and management responsibility. The increased premium flexibility for the new generation of life insurance policies coupled with periods of low interest rates, has heightened the possibility that, without management, the coverage may not last as long as it needs to last. An ongoing advisor relationship will be needed.

Future Regrets That Were Avoided

- The lapse of a valuable life insurance policy

- The lapse of needed life insurance due to large policy loans

Real Estate Gone South

Phil is a retired actuary and understands how life insurance works perhaps better than any other client that we have. He retired early and made some investments in commercial real estate. As sometimes happens, the expenses were greater than expected and the occupancy was lower than expected. Then, the balloon note with the bank became due. Added to the mix was the fact that the appraisal would not justify the new loan needed. The bank asked for cash in order to make the loan-to-value ratios work.

Phil and his wife Sally own several lots adjacent to their home. So, they decided to borrow $250,000 based upon the value of these lots in order to make the commercial property loans happen. Time passed, and eventually Phil accepted the fact that everything was now underwater. When the real estate decisions were being made, everything made sense. Based upon past experiences, the steps were reasonable. But unfortunately, there are times when seemingly wise decisions, in hindsight, prove later to be missteps because of unforeseen circumstances.

Phil owns a life insurance policy that has a guaranteed death benefit as long as the premiums are paid. We had been following the progress of this policy because some of the premium payments had been skipped because of cash flow difficulties. He needed to adjust his premiums in order to make up for the past premiums that he had missed.

The unsolicited e-mail note below expresses Phil's feelings after our review:

> Gary,
>
> It was really nice talking to you two weeks ago. Thank you for your help.
>
> As I told you, if I couldn't pay anything else, I would pay the premium on my life insurance policy. The policy is the only way I can leave Sally enough money to pay off our mortgages and live comfortably the rest of her life, which is more than I've been able to do while I'm living. She will have the option of paying off the mortgages, or investing the proceeds and using the income for the mortgage payments.
>
> Seven years ago, when I got with you to improve my life insurance, the process resulted in one of the best financial decisions I've ever made. The plan guarantees that Sally will have a meaningful sum of money when I die.
>
> Sally and I both know that when I die she can count on you to help guide her through the many decisions that will be facing her.
>
> Thank you so much,
> Phil

When people make decisions, especially financial decisions, they usually think whatever they're about to do is a good idea. Unfortunately, things don't always work out as planned. It's likely that most of us can cite examples from our own lives where this has happened. It's one thing to experience difficulties personally, but when the pain can extend to others you care about, the dynamic gets worse.

Future Regrets That Were Avoided:

- Financial hardship for Sally

- Possible loss of family home due to debts

GENERATIONAL IMPACT

Committing Time and Resources to Planning Creates Relationship Value

When I think of legacy, I think of something left behind that's tangible or possibly just a memory or feeling of what a person was like. The stories presented in this section represent many who make plans and apply resources to protect and provide for those they love. The steps taken will be noticed and felt by the survivors, who may extend beyond one or two generations.

AVOIDABLE REGRET

Missed Opportunity to Help Others

Leaving a spouse, family, or business with untenable financial choices clearly adds complexity to an already stressful transition. The transition might include adjusting to being alone, and include financial responsibility for many unknown future events. The extended survivors may feel this pain as well.

BEGIN WITH A VISION OF THE DESIRED END RESULT

"The beginning is the most important
part of any work."

– Plato

A Vision of the Future

I was sitting at the conference table in my office one day with Henry, who is a friend and has been a client for over twenty years. We were reflecting on how well things have progressed over the years and thinking through some plans for the next phase of his life.

He owns a successful business as well as other assets including a second home at Sea Island, Georgia. He has a wife and two adult children. One child works in the business and the other is a homemaker. Henry loves his family, his business that he created and built, and the home at Sea Island. He wanted to make some plans so that a train wreck does not occur with any of these important aspects of his life. He made the comment that "all of this success" creates a lot of complexity.

The conversation led me to ask Henry a high-level question. I asked him to fast-forward twenty years and describe for me what success for all of this might look like. He stared out the window for a moment and then he stared at the ceiling. All the while, I remained quiet, and he finally said, "Twenty years from now, when my kids get together at Christmas, I would like for them to like each other." This is a very reasonable high-level answer, and it gave us a place to start and the beginning of a creative solution.

One of the most difficult, yet most important steps, of the estate planning process is the visualization of how the plan might ultimately unfold. That is, considering the way all of one's assets are titled along with the flow of the distributions to heirs according to the legal documents, what is the long-term picture going to look like? And, is that outcome wanted?

All of these questions, along with others, are the reason why the front-end conversations with the planning team are so important. While parts of the conversation may be awkward to discuss, the team will understand your desires better and be in a better position to help. The process begins with the vision.

There may be a desire to keep the property within the family bloodline. There may be specific desires related to a closely held business. There may be a desire to leave assets to support a specific cause that's important to the individual.

Keeping It in the Family

Jay and Jane's family is a classic example that illustrates the process of thinking through and making plans to accomplish the desired end result. The family includes three grown and married children who are all self-supporting. Jay and Jane have three valuable illiquid assets: a closely held business, a unique family home, and a collection of residential rental properties.

For the foreseeable future their objective is to keep all these properties within the family. Naturally, there are also other assets such as a retirement plan, some undeveloped real estate, and a second home in the mountains of North Carolina.

Since their three children have gotten married and have evolved into three young married couples, Jay and Jane want to rethink their estate plan so that their legacy assets will remain in their bloodline. That is, to avoid property that's left to an adult child being possibly lost and transferred outside the family due to either the child's death, divorce, or some other unforeseen circumstance. We helped them think through the possible scenarios. They like their in-laws, but they know that marriages can fail, people can change, and surprises can happen.

A primary objective for Jay and Jane was to first provide for their own financial security. Close behind this initial objective is thinking through the doomsday scenario, which is what happens if they both die simultaneously, or when the second spouse dies. Because of the personalities involved, it would not make sense for the three siblings to own all the properties jointly.

Let's consider the three legacy properties and call the three children Child 1, Child 2, and Child 3. First, let's think through the plan for the closely held business. Child 1 presently works in the business. He is very perceptive, and has pointed out that if mom and dad both die he could be in a tough spot. If all three children own the business equally and together, then the other two inactive siblings can fire, or at least control, the one that's working and devoted to the business. This is hardly an ideal arrangement.

The family business has been the engine that has provided the family support and created the other assets over the years. If both mom and dad pass away and Child 1 inherits the business outright and then gets divorced, the former spouse may then own a portion of the business as a part of the divorce settlement. Child 1 would likely have to find a way to compensate the former spouse in order to avoid the likely unpleasant experience of owning a business with the ex-spouse.

On the other hand, what if Child 1 dies prematurely? The business ownership may then pass to the surviving spouse and it may be that she has no interest in running the business or lacks the skills necessary to do so. Furthermore, the surviving spouse may remarry. None of these scenarios are attractive.

Next, consider the family home which has been within the family for three generations and is a very special place. Child 2 has circumstances that make ownership of this property attractive. What happens if Child 2 dies or gets divorced? It becomes doubtful that this family legacy property will remain within the family bloodline without some planning.

Child 3 has life circumstances and skills that make owning the residential rental properties attractive. But again, without planning the death or divorce of Child 3, it may cause these valuable properties to exit the family's ownership and control.

With the backdrop of these scenarios in mind, Jay and Jane considered each of the options after talking it through with their advisory planning team. It had been noted that they have three children and three primary legacy assets. So, the decision was made to create three separate trusts to hold the properties should both parents die. A trust for each of the three children was created, and each trust would hold the one legacy asset that was most appropriate for that particular child.

The family business would go into one trust for the child that was active in the business. The family home, a unique property, would go into a trust for the second child. The residential rental properties would go into a trust for the third child.

Each child would be the trustee of their own trust along with a co-trustee. The co-trustee had powers, but also served as a mentor and a protector who would have some discretion related to the duration of the trust as well as his own involvement. The trustee was about ten years younger than Jay and Jane.

A significant part of this arrangement provided that if a child died, the assets in his or her trust would revert to the surviving siblings. Because of the value of these properties and the young age of the three adult children, Jay and Jane felt this was the most appropriate solution for now. They understood that the plan could be changed later if they wished to do so.

As you might expect, the value of each of the three trusts containing the legacy assets would not be equal. So, the tax-free cash proceeds from an existing life insurance trust, along with the other estate assets, could be used to pay estate taxes and equalize, as much as possible, the value of each child's inheritance upon the death of the last surviving parent.

Future Regrets That Were Avoided

- Joint ownership of the legacy properties by the siblings may have caused relationship stress and business complexity

- The possibility of legacy properties leaving the family bloodline

- Having to sell legacy assets

- Leaving an unequal inheritance to heirs

The One Last Standing Decides

Virgil and Martha never planned to annoy their extended family but it happened anyway. They were married for sixty-two years and never had children. But, they both came from rather large families and had younger siblings and lots of nieces and nephews.

They lived frugally all of those years and both had careers. They never considered themselves wealthy because it all happened so slowly. Furthermore, when they looked at their accumulated assets they never felt like their nest egg was large enough because, after all, they "might get sick" and need it.

They never engaged in any sort of estate planning process because in their minds, they just had each other. And, they each had a simple will which left everything to the survivor. They were also private people and reluctant to discuss their financial affairs. They had grown up during the Great Depression and that's just the way they were.

Ultimately, Virgil was stricken with cancer and died after a brief illness. Whatever he owned, which included home ownership, investments, personal effects, and family heirlooms, went to Martha.

Martha died about a year later and all of the assets that Virgil and Martha had owned together and accumulated passed to her side of the family. Maybe this was the way they had planned. But, if they had considered the end result, they might have preferred a different outcome.

The end result was that Virgil's siblings felt left out of the process. After all, Virgil was their brother, and everything— including his personal effects and some family heirlooms— passing to Martha's side of the family just didn't feel right. It wasn't so much about the money as it was about the principle involved.

It's doubtful this outcome was what Virgil, or Martha, wanted. Whether the result was intentional or simply an oversight will never be known. The heirs of the last spouse to die received everything by default.

Regret That Could Have Been Avoided

- Virgil's siblings felt disinherited and forgotten

GENERATIONAL IMPACT

Unique Circumstances Require Intentional Planning

Living on with an inherited set of circumstances is likely to be palatable if you know that the plan was a thoroughly considered best alternative. The circumstances may not be perfect, but at least there was a reason for it. Younger generations are impacted financially as well as emotionally by the plans set in motion by the older family members.

AVOIDABLE REGRET

Unintended Negative Consequences

Legacy properties passing to strangers or disgruntled in-laws is a result that most wish to avoid. Living a successful life with rewarding relationships and a healthy degree of pride related to having lived well can be tainted by a disorganized exit from our worldly affairs. More importantly, those that we love the most can be hurt—not just financially, but emotionally as well.

KNOW THAT THE SMALL DETAILS ARE IMPORTANT

"Give me six hours to chop down a tree and I will spend the first four sharpening the axe."

– Abraham Lincoln

The Small Stuff

One of my older friends in the Marietta Rotary Club, a high-level corporate executive and a past president of the club, told me once that the difference between being "first-class" and being "good" is in the small details. That is, those details that might be considered to be small stuff.

Our lives today are busy and complicated. Setting aside time to get it right regarding the details of our planning is wise. Planning when some sort of "event" happens is not the ideal setting.

It's human nature to be most creative when we are relaxing and listening to the waves crash against the beach, or when our backs are against the wall and we are in some sort of panic. Our lives being what they are, most of our time is spent at neither of those two places. As a result, important decisions are sometimes deferred.

It takes wisdom to make plans for the future because, while it's very important, it's usually not urgent. None of us are immortal, so we do well to remember the following:

> "Teach us to number our days, that we may gain a heart of wisdom."

> – Psalms 90:12

I received a call one evening at home from Stanley who is a dentist. He said that he was in the hospital and was scheduled to have brain surgery the next morning. He asked if I would come to the hospital that evening to meet with him and his wife, Janice. They wanted to review the details related to his life and disability insurance. I did go, and was happy to do so.

With Stanley, we had periodic reviews annually but Janice had never been present. So, on the night before his surgery the details were reassuring to that family. In Stanley's case, the brain issue was a blood clot that was successfully healed. On other occasions, I've received calls from hospital patients asking if I could arrange for an estate planning attorney to visit them and assist with legal aspects of their estate plan. Discussing and executing legal documents in a hospital room is not the ideal setting, but it happens.

There's a Reason for the Process

James was somewhat of a mystery. He was referred to me by his CPA and he came to our office for the initial visit. We are relationship oriented and prefer not to do transactions for people, but James knew what he wanted to do so we put into place a $250,000 life insurance policy with his wife being the beneficiary.

Three or four years later, he called and said he would like to add an additional $250,000 policy and afterward he came to our office to complete the application. Once the underwriting process was completed, he returned to review the policy and we let him know that he did not receive the best underwriting class, as he did on the first policy, because he had gained weight. The increased premium for the new policy was not that significant but he decided to decline the insurance company's offer because he wanted to lose the extra weight and try again a little later.

This story does not end well. A few months later, on a foggy day in the mountains of Tennessee, he and his wife both died in a plane crash. Our client was the pilot even though he had made no mention of flying, and in fact, had indicated on the second application that he was not a pilot. He must've considered this to be a small detail, when in fact it was an important piece of information that needed to be disclosed.

The original policy was beyond the twenty-four month contestability period. They had no children and the proceeds from the initial $250,000 policy were paid to his estate.

As it turned out, James owned a portion of a small business. The end result could have been much better had James shared with me what he was thinking and allowed us to have a conversation about the bigger picture. This experience hardened our firm's resolve against handling insurance transactions for individuals without first engaging them in our planning process.

Because of the circumstances involved, I was not privy to a lot of the details but I do know that the insurance proceeds ultimately went to James's parents. They lived out of state and they had the unwieldy chore of negotiating the sale of James's interest in the closely held business.

The business struggled because of the settlement related to the purchase of James's interest. James's parents had no desire to be a minority owner of the business since they lived out of state and had no knowledge of the business's operation. Compounding the financial predicament of the business was the necessity of replacing the talent that James contributed to the success of the operation.

Regret That Could Have Been Avoided

- Lack of detailed conversation and planning created complexity for parents and hardship for surviving business partners

A Happy and Surprised Ex-Wife

Few people periodically review their life insurance beneficiary designations. Most just don't think about it. They're not planning to die anytime soon and taking the time for such a review does not make it onto the "to do" list, but the details of planning are important.

Carey was divorced and had recently remarried. He died unexpectedly, and his bride who was now a widow, came by our office. She asked if there is a way to "fix" the beneficiary designation on Carey's life insurance policy that was directed to his ex-wife. Unfortunately, there was no way we could help her. Obviously, Carey could not review the policy posthumously. The fact that Carey and his ex-wife had a nasty divorce didn't matter. The ex-wife was the policy beneficiary.

It also didn't matter that the new wife was sure that he would have wanted her to receive the check for more than $500,000. In the end, it was a very good day for the ex-wife. Who knows, maybe that was Carey's intention all along, but I doubt it.

The purpose of a beneficiary designation is for the policy owner to indicate where the proceeds are to be directed. Therefore, the designation should be carefully considered and if a change is desired, the proper procedure needs to be followed. In addition to a primary beneficiary, it's important to designate a contingent beneficiary that will receive the proceeds if the primary beneficiary is deceased.

All of the various pieces of the estate plan, including the life insurance, need to "talk to each other" and be coordinated. For example, it's possible to have a high dollar and well thought out legal estate plan involving an appropriate will and possibly some trusts that contemplate funding by life insurance policies. But, if the life insurance policy beneficiary is an individual, then the cash proceeds go directly to that individual and bypass the well thought out plan created by the legal documents.

In our practice, we have seen situations where wills and trusts were implemented and written, as well as verbal, instructions given by the attorney were never followed. Changes were recommended regarding how property should be titled, and how life insurance policy beneficiaries should be designated, but the changes were never made.

This means that major assets can pass directly to others and bypass the carefully created legal estate plan. The intentions were good but the follow-through was poor and the individual's plans failed to be properly implemented.

Regret That Could Have Been Avoided

- The ex-wife received the insurance death proceeds instead of the current wife

The Hazards of Crossing the Street

It's not advisable to make a minor child the beneficiary of a life insurance policy. We advise our corporate clients who offer group life insurance to periodically ask all of their employees to review and possibly complete a new beneficiary designation for their group life coverage.

About twenty-five years ago, one of my first corporate clients provided group life insurance to their employees. Linda, one of the covered employees, was hit by a car and killed crossing Peachtree Street in downtown Atlanta as she was headed to the bank. She was young, divorced, and had a small child.

After her divorce, she changed her beneficiary designation to her child who was maybe three or four years old at the time. The employer provided her with the form and it was completed, submitted directly to the insurance company, and recorded.

A protracted legal battle took place after her death. Both the child's father, who was Linda's ex-husband, and Linda's parents stepped in and attempted to claim the proceeds on behalf of the child. Since the death was caused by an accident, the proceeds were over $500,000.

I was not involved with the dispute, which was eventually worked out by the court system, and I don't know what transpired. But the complexity that followed was unfortunate and could have been prevented.

This painful process was in addition to Linda's parents losing their daughter, and Linda's child losing her mother. Linda understandably wasn't expecting to get hit by a car on the way to the bank. The outcome would've been better if the detail of naming a minor child as the primary beneficiary had been thoroughly considered. When a death claim occurs, it's too late to change the beneficiary.

Early on in my college experience at Georgia Tech, I learned that over-preparation and attention to detail was a good thing. Being underprepared and inattentive with the details was expensive. There were times after a test when I remembered that I knew how to solve the problem all along, but I just missed it on the test. When the professor collected the papers, the test was over and the scores would be recorded. There was no opportunity to go back and make changes. This concept applies to many aspects of life.

Regret That Could Have Been Avoided

- Linda's parents engaged in a legal battle with her ex-husband over her child's financial provision

GENERATIONAL IMPACT

Unintended Oversights Can Circumvent Well-Made Plans

The confusion and misdirection of assets caused by overlooked details that are not buttoned-up can create hardship for survivors. Valuable assets may flow to people and entities where this was not the intention.

AVOIDABLE REGRET

Legal Fights Caused by Mistakes

When someone dies, from a legal standpoint, their business affairs are largely driven by the existing paper documents. They need to be organized and correct because the deceased will not be around to fix or explain anything. The opportunity to have a graceful exit will have been missed.

BE REALISTIC
WHEN PLANNING
FOR FUTURE NEEDS

"Create your future from your future, not your past."

– Werner Erhard

Regardless of the size of the estate or net worth, I've never known anyone who did not need some amount of continuing income to support their lifestyle. If one is independently wealthy, they have assets or income created by some source that pays their bills.

Financial projections can be created that make certain assumptions for future investment returns, inflation, and needs. Then a present value analysis can be performed to determine whether or not sufficient assets are in place to support the future need.

If additional capital is needed to support the future need, life insurance can be implemented, if health status permits, to fill the gap. Along this line, if one's future income is dependent upon work related employment, then plans should be considered to replace this income if a disability occurs.

It's Important That Disability Plans Work

Disability insurance has a lot of fine print outlining the definitions and the circumstances under which the insurance company will pay a claim. The strength of these definitions for new policies has largely been reduced over the last fifteen or twenty years.

Therefore, extra care is necessary when an insurance carrier and policy are selected. It's important to go beyond the monthly benefit indicated on the cover page of an individual policy or the formula for income replacement on a group disability policy.

A friend and client called me one Sunday afternoon and asked if I would help a friend of his. He had just gotten off the phone with Michael, who is a neurosurgeon at a large medical center in the Northeast. Michael had been battling depression for a while and was considering taking some time off in order to heal. He had some disability coverage through his employer and coverage provided by some older policies that were implemented when he was in private practice.

My mission was to help him understand the benefits related to mental and nervous conditions so that he could better sort through his options. I called Michael that afternoon and let them know that I would be happy to help and described to him what I would need in order to get started. He was in a difficult position because he did not want to go to human resources and discuss his situation because he was afraid it might damage his career.

As is typical of busy professionals, he was unfamiliar with the coverage provided by his employer, although he was aware that something was in place for both short-term and long-term disability benefits. I asked him to contact human resources and ask for electronic copies of the contracts related to these various disability plans so that he could provide them to me. I also asked him to send copies of his individual policies.

A couple of days later, we received electronic copies of his employer-provided coverage and received his individual policies by overnight mail. As it turns out, his group disability policy had a maximum benefit of $15,000 per month, but unfortunately, claims for mental and nervous conditions were limited to a maximum duration of twelve months.

The short-term disability policy had no limitations on mental and nervous conditions and would pay $18,000 per month beginning after thirty days of being disabled as defined in the policy. It had a maximum benefit period of sixty days, which was when the long-term disability policy began payments if he was still disabled.

In addition, an individual disability policy with a $2,500 per month benefit was provided by his employer, but this policy had a twenty-four month limitation on mental and nervous conditions.

As it turned out, the only long-term policies that fully covered mental nervous conditions were his individual policies, with a total benefit of $7,500 per month. But, the $7,500 monthly benefit from these was inadequate to support the needs for his family since his total annual income was approximately $800,000.

These policies had been in place for fifteen or twenty years. The broker who helped with these policies was retired.

Michael's confidence in his ability to make a decision increased once he possessed the facts. He was concerned about what he called the "slippery slope" of going out on a short-term disability claim.

For higher income individuals, particularly those with narrow fields of specialty, often the standard group disability program is more of a detriment than a help. The definitions of disability are often woefully weak and opting out of the coverage is not typically allowed by the employer.

Because $15,000 per month of group disability coverage may be in place, this amount is subtracted from what might otherwise be possible to obtain with a new individual policy. The underwriters for the individual coverage do not want their insured individual to be over-insured and possibly lack the incentive to return to work. In other words, the existence of the group plan may prohibit the individual from obtaining a specialty specific policy with comprehensive coverage.

Over the years, the pure cost of life insurance has declined because of improved life expectancy due, in part, to our access to high-quality health care. The flip side of this is that we're living longer and the cost of disability and long-term care insurance has been increasing.

If you think about it, a life insurance claim is relatively simple to administer. For the insurance company, the question of whether or not the person is alive can be determined.

For disability income insurance plans however, the financial model can be adjusted for new applicants by both changing the premiums and modifying the contractual provisions that determine whether or not a covered claim exists. Therefore, the consideration of any of these plans requires significant attention to detail. The plans are not commodities that are easily compared.

Future Regret That Was Avoided

- A review of the current disability income insurance, prior to a decision about the future being made, prevented unpleasant surprises later

A Visit from the Wife

Steve was a member of the staff at a well-known church in Atlanta. He was diagnosed with a progressive disease that would likely cause him to eventually be disabled. The church provided no disability insurance and the administration was concerned about Steve and his family's financial future.

One of my friends was on the finance committee at the church and called me and asked if there were any solutions. Their current insurance broker had indicated that nothing could be done.

After some conversation, we installed a group disability program for all the employees that required no medical questions. The plan did, however, include a provision that required Steve to work for at least twelve months after the plan started prior to becoming disabled in order to qualify for future disability payments.

After about three years, Steve could no longer work. He filed a claim and began receiving sixty percent of his income that would be payable until age sixty-five as long as his disability continued. Since he was in his mid forties at the time of claim, the total benefit was significant.

I've never met Steve, but I'll never forget meeting his wife, Patricia. She came to my office one day because she wanted to meet me and thank me. She said the check they receive each month gives them dignity that they otherwise would be unable to have.

Future Regret That Was Avoided

- Loss of dignity, and the ability to support the family, due to loss of income

A Continuing Need for Capital

Bill and Elizabeth continue to think of themselves as being young even though they are in their early sixties. They are young at heart, like to travel, and continue to dream about their plans for the future. They bought an expensive second home on a South Carolina beach a couple of years ago.

They are optimistic about the future, but troubled by the continued memory of how it felt when their retirement plan assets dropped significantly a few years ago. Another concern is that part of Bill's retirement income will be reduced after he turns seventy-five.

Their retirement plan has mostly recovered, but there's a concern that volatility may happen again because of uncertainty in the world and the political landscape at home. Another concern is that the type of life insurance they have is not designed to last much longer. Bill is an executive with a large public company and understands that when he retires his group life insurance, which is substantial, will cease to exist. Elizabeth doesn't like the idea of having no life insurance beyond the next few years.

Bill and Elizabeth asked us to help them sort through their life insurance choices, and because of their age, health status, and objectives, we recommended a portfolio approach to continue some coverage on Bill's life. By "portfolio approach," I'm referring to the use of multiple policies, each with a specific purpose. For example, there may be a certain amount of coverage that is designed to last for life. There's an additional layer designed to last into his seventies and an additional layer designed to last the next few years.

The predominant fears and dangers our clients seem to focus on frequently include the dissipation of their current assets due to bad decisions, taxation, or simply a bad economy. They're also concerned about the prospect of running out of money due to an extended lifetime that may include expensive care.

Future Regrets That Were Avoided

- Forecasting and solving future security needs reduced the possibility of financial strain in the future

GENERATIONAL IMPACT

Inadequate Income Affects
More Than Just Paying the Bills

A shortage of income caused by a disability, loss of capital, or any other reason can become a game changer. The repercussions of this vibrate throughout the family because of the psychological impact of the stress related to a reduced lifestyle.

AVOIDABLE REGRET

Inadequate Income

Being forced to reduce one's lifestyle at any point in life is disturbing. It's particularly troubling later in life because of the inability to reinvent yourself or create income through employment. Securing dignity during the last stage of life requires planning. Planning after it's really too late is often fruitless because the options are limited.

DO NO HARM BY PROVIDING TOO LITTLE OR TOO MUCH

"Wisdom, like an inheritance, is a good thing…"

– Ecclesiastes 7:11a

The Right Number

I believe parents, for the most part, want their offspring to make it on their own and be responsible for their own future. I've never heard anyone say they want to enrich their kids so that they really won't have to work or be concerned about financial provision for the rest of their lives. Leaving too much unstructured wealth too early can be harmful. Similarly, leaving too little can be harmful. A process to determine the appropriate number is a place to begin.

As clients become older, many become less concerned about leaving "too much" to their families. I believe the reason for this is complex. Somewhere in the mix, there may be factors such as an improved relationship with adult children, seeing their grandchildren begin to develop, as well as concerns about how the world is changing from an economic and political standpoint.

How much is enough is often a part of the life insurance conversation. Over the years, I've delivered life insurance proceeds to beneficiaries in a wide range of circumstances. I've rarely thought the amount was too much, but I've delivered many checks that I thought were too small.

The older generation realizes that the world their children and grandchildren will experience will be much different from theirs. Thinking through the possibility of private school tuition, the unknown consequences of future economies, along with other factors, tends to influence their opinion.

I believe most of the wealthy individuals with whom I've had the pleasure to work, both self-made and with inherited wealth, would like to give the gift of wisdom and confidence to their offspring that is a by-product of having made it on their own. Wisdom and confidence often develop from dealing with and surviving struggles.

Wrestling with the right balance can be a challenge. Few want the "fruits of their labor" created over their lifetime to be misused. I believe that we are born with an instinct that wants to preserve and move forward, in a positive way, what we have initiated during our lives.

When passing along our accumulated property, there are only a few choices. When we look at our net worth statements we can think to ourselves, *I'm either going to lose this, give it away to charity, leave it to my heirs, or allow the government to take part of it and use it for public purposes.* Our grip on it will cease and whatever is passed along to our heirs will have a significant effect on them—positive or negative.

I believe the strong preference is to leave assets so that they will be used to provide a level of security, opportunity, and possibly to further some cause or belief that is dearly held. This may involve philanthropy. It may involve the promotion of dreams held by younger family members. But, for ultra-high net worth families, there may be an underlying fear that somehow their provision may harm those who are fortunate enough to receive it.

A Scene I'll Never Forget

Early in my career, when I was maybe twenty-five years old, I was allowed to sit in on a meeting that I still vividly remember. At the time, the subject was far beyond anything that I could help with, but a gentleman had stopped by to visit with an older and wiser mentor of mine to discuss estate planning. The visitor was maybe in his mid-fifties, which at the time I thought was an advanced age. He had just sold his business and received $15 million net after taxes.

As he began to talk and tell his story, he became emotional and started weeping. Personally, as a struggling young entrepreneur, it was hard for me to imagine anyone crying after just netting $15 million in cash. But, he was worried about his children. They were young adults, some close to my age at the time, and he was concerned about what the money, without structure, might do to them when he and his wife passed away.

As a side note, I didn't then realize the full range of emotions that this man was experiencing. For starters, when a business is begun, there's no assurance that it will succeed. There's risk involved, along with some lean times financially, in addition to long hours and a lot of hard work. The dream of what it might become motivates the founder to keep moving ahead, and in a way the business becomes his child.

The later sale of this dream, or child if you will, can be traumatic. The founder wonders what he will do next. He wonders how his identity will be affected. The family is plunged into a transition in the community and among themselves.

He was a wise man who loved his children, and he didn't know what to do. I was a newlywed at the time and had no children, but listening to that conversation opened my eyes. I remember him saying that he did not want to "ruin" his children.

He was familiar with Proverbs 20:21, "An inheritance claimed too soon will not be blessed at the end." This wise man was looking back over his adult life and evaluating whether or not the values he had tried to instill in his children had been transferred and accepted. He had some regrets as I recall, as most of us do.

He wanted his children to be motivated, ambitious, and experience the meaning that comes from being productive. Sigmund Freud said that the two greatest sources of a happy integrated human life were for an individual to learn to love and to work, with work defined as a calling.

An advisory planning team was created for this gentleman and his wife. They were guided through a process that helped them create a structure to protect the family assets, as well as a process to prepare and protect the heirs. Philanthropy was also a part of the plan.

Future Regret That Was Avoided

- Leaving too much unstructured wealth to heirs too early might have been harmful

James E. Hughes Jr. in his book *Family Wealth—Keeping it in the Family,* distinguishes between a gift and a transfer. He writes that a gift enhances the human and intellectual development of another. On the other hand, a transfer might initiate the downhill slide of another into the state of victimhood known as entitlement.[2]

In other words, it's really better to help someone develop their talent as a fisherman rather than simply giving them a fish. There's an innate reward in knowing that you have caught your own fish, and it is a totally different feeling when a fish is given to you.

Leaving no money but passing values to heirs is acceptable because they will likely manage their lives well. Leaving money and passing values to heirs is usually a positive situation because they will likely thrive and be productive. Leaving money to heirs who have poorly developed values may hurt more than it helps. Having assets and people in your life that you love creates responsibility.

---

[2] James E. Hughes Jr., *Family Wealth—Keeping it in the Family,* (New York: Bloomberg, 2004).

The Development of Competency

Being unprepared to receive a large sum of money usually does not end well. I saw an article in *Sports Illustrated* magazine indicating that 78 percent of NFL players were broke within three years after retirement. Similarly, 60 percent of NBA players were bankrupt five years after leaving the league. Money can be a significant blessing to the recipient if they are prepared and possess the maturity to handle it. But, personal development and growth can be stalled if too much money is received too early. This can harm the one that it may have been meant to help.

Determining how much to leave a beneficiary is a very personal decision. There are no formulas. I believe that planning oriented towards the reduction of taxes should come after consideration has been given to the effect that the financial inheritance, or lack thereof, would have on individual family members. You might say this approach is consistent with the "first, do no harm" philosophy.

The concern about leaving too much too early and how that might affect the beneficiary's behavior is a concern of most clients. For inheritances, it is quite common to authorize distributions at certain ages such as age twenty-five, thirty, and thirty-five. The idea behind these staggered distributions is that if the beneficiary makes mistakes early on there will be opportunities to do better next time.

We learn from our struggles and many times this is gradual, but when too much is done for an individual too early, there is limited opportunity to appropriately grow in wisdom. In a way, it's almost as though each generation of the family needs to possess some of the characteristics of the first, wealth-creating generation. Some family members may not have a clue as to how difficult it is to create a business or wealth.

Soon after I began my career, I heard the phrase "control from the grave" which was referring to trusts and various techniques to have financial controls in place after one passes on. An experienced planning team can lead one through a process of determining balance between leaving too little, "controlling from the grave," and leaving so much freedom that it actually hurts those left behind.

An Offer That Was Declined

I've noticed that sometimes the motivation to plan comes too late. Roger contacted me to inquire about the possibility of obtaining life insurance because of the lack of financial security for his family. During the initial conversation, I learned that he had a congenital heart defect, but was doing well.

A medical history like this is a detriment to obtaining life insurance, but we were able to obtain an offer for him anyway although the premium was increased because of his history. Roger and his wife Sandra considered the offer and declined.

About three years later, Roger died. I later learned that their mortgage lender ultimately foreclosed on their home loan, and Sandra lost the home. Sandra, in her early fifties, returned to the job market. The story would be quite different had they accepted the life insurance offer.

Regret That Could Have Been Avoided

- The family home was lost and the surviving spouse experienced financial stress

An Untimely Death

Tony and Jerry were brothers and owned a business that was begun by their father back in the 1930s. Businesses have to change with the times, otherwise they run the risk of becoming obsolete. Innovation does not come easily when you're in your sixties and you've had a comfortable lifestyle and stable business for many years.

Tony and Jerry were one of my first business clients where the owners were significantly older than I was. They each had $250,000 of life insurance that was designed to last for their lifetime combined with $750,000 of term life insurance.

By design, the term insurance policy had a premium that increased significantly after twenty years when they were in their late sixties. When the premium increased, they discontinued the term insurance policy as their business was not doing well because of outside competitive forces.

When the brothers were in their early seventies, their business had declined to the point where their only choice was to close it. About six months later, Tony had a stroke as he was lying in his recliner at home and died.

Shortly thereafter, I delivered the check for the $250,000 policy to his widow. She was young and vibrant for her age, and I recall thinking that she might live for an additional twenty years or so. The additional $750,000 would've made a big difference to her future had they accepted the recommendation to continue the additional insurance.

Regret That Could Have Been Avoided

* Financial reversals later in life can happen resulting in too little cash left for survivors

GENERATIONAL IMPACT

Too Much or Too Little—Both Can Be Damaging

A death in the family and the settlement of the estate is a process that may bring significant change to the survivors. A lifestyle change may ensue and it may be positive or negative.

AVOIDABLE REGRET

Inadequate Preparation

Leaving too little to survivors, without preparation, may leave them vulnerable. Leaving too much, without preparation, may be harmful.

CREATE A CULTURE WHERE VALUES AND WISDOM ARE TRANSFERRED

"Coming together is a beginning, staying together is progress, and working together is success."

– Henry Ford

In a perfect world, in which none of us live, we would each have a deliberate and early plan to transfer our values and wisdom to the next generation. This transfer is easier said than done because we're dealing with other human beings. It's a delicate process and usually takes time. The incubation period for the seeds that are planted may extend beyond our lifetimes.

Starting Early Is Best

Children pick up traits and habits from their parents that they will probably pass along in some form to the next generation. I've observed that a family who possesses common positive values has a distinct advantage related to the successful management of family property, as well as the settlement of the parents' estates.

Recently, Melissa and I became grandparents. It has made me recall some of the same thoughts I had many years ago when our children were born. Although I still have a lot to learn, I wish I could somehow instantly transmit to our grandson's core being some files that contain all that I've learned so far about life, people, and everything else.

I wish I could give him a head start on the process because for most of us the journey is slow and sometimes painful. I believe that one effective way to promote the effort is philanthropy.

My observation is that, for most of us, our wealth of knowledge is gained by plodding, unspectacular steps. But I believe most responsible parents wish their descendants could "see what they see" and attempt along the way to provide direction. An early start is best.

A Video Clip That's Still in My Head

Parents and grandparents who emphasize offering assistance to causes they are passionate about will model their values to younger family members. This will contribute to their increased value of themselves as leaders and contributors.

My father was a debit life insurance agent, which means he had a section of town for which he was responsible for servicing and collecting the premiums for relatively small life insurance policies. Many of his customers at the time were underprivileged and some lived in public housing. Because of this, he was aware of needs within the community and developed relationships with folks in varying walks of life.

I have a video clip in my brain that I can still extract and see from an evening when I was probably six or seven years old. It was Christmas Eve and our tradition was to visit my grandmother. After we arrived at my grandmother's home, my dad pulled me aside and directed me to come along with him. Somehow, he had gotten the message that there was a family nearby that had no food. I don't know how he received the message, but I do remember going into a little apartment in public housing.

I remember how it smelled, and I remember there were a couple of female adults there along with two or three young children who all were about my age. I recall thinking that I was dressed up for a party, and they were not. There was no Christmas tree there.

I can still see my father confidently walking into that apartment and into the kitchen where he began to look in the cabinets that were empty. We went to a small grocery store near the Marietta Square, named Kirk's Market at the time, and bought some supplies and returned to the apartment.

I don't remember anything that was said that night but I clearly recall what I saw happen.

Living in a Village Helps

During many years of working with families and their financial matters, I have observed that a grandparent's relationship with his or her grandchildren is filled with pure love. Grandparents and grandchildren are often natural buddies.

The relationship offers the opportunity to teach the younger family members positive values without the parental obligation of being concerned with discipline and other complicated dynamics of the immediate family.

Philanthropy, as an ongoing discovery project for the older and younger generations, is a great teaching tool to use for learning virtues through the process of giving to others. God has crafted each of our personalities, temperaments, life situations, passions, and callings in a unique way. A framework might include the following:

1. A donor-advised fund can be created even with a relatively small amount of money. The fund may be hosted by a local community foundation or some other convenient source.

2. Grandparents and grandchildren form a grants committee and allow each grandchild to make a cash grant each year.

3. As a part of the grant making process, the older grandchildren—perhaps ages ten and up—should be capable of proposing and advocating a gift request at an annual meeting.

4. Handson training in philanthropy including site visits to the proposed grantee or an interview with the director of the organization can be arranged.

From the grandparent's perspective, what could be more fun than to sit with one's grandchildren, discuss their passions, and learn about them? From a grandchild's standpoint, what could be more beneficial than getting to make discoveries about the world and its needs, and most importantly getting to know the hearts of the grandparents along with their wisdom obtained by living for a few decades?

I know of one family that gave their young teenage children $300 each and asked them to give the money away over the next six months and report back on how the money was used and how it felt to give it away. One child became aware of a friend's family in need because the father had lost his job. An anonymous money order was placed in an envelope and left in the family's mailbox. The other child contributed to making it possible for a needy friend to attend summer church youth camp. Developing empathy for others and learning early how it feels to help others is boosted by hands-on learning experiences. Mailing checks is not as effective as hands-on engagement.

Ingredients That Make Sense

Personally, I've observed three ingredients that are usually present with most effective plans for philanthropy:

1. **Passion**—there may be a life experience that has inspired or somehow shaped the perspective of the donors. On a fundamental level, philanthropy is about being a caregiver. It involves caring about others and somehow identifying with them and wanting to help. It's sort of a "that could be me" feeling. Or, a feeling that "I want to help others because I have been there."

2. **Do for one what you wish you could do for everyone**— wiping out illiteracy worldwide is a nice thought, but it's

overwhelming. But, what about helping one child with a learning disability?

If a need has not been identified, it's okay. A significant advantage of a donor-advised fund is that the contribution can be made now, along with the enjoyment of the tax advantages, and decisions can be made later about making disbursements.

3. **Go deep, not wide**—needs within any community are abundant, so having some established giving parameters is wise. Family members might be asked to list causes they care about the most. The list might include education, faith, health care, the arts, and others. A consensus may emerge around a few core principles that might shape the focus for the family philanthropy effort.

I'm convinced that discovering and pursuing one's calling along with the source of personal fulfillment is more important than accumulating money. The desire for meaning and genuine connection with others will always transcend accumulated wealth.

Motivation Is a Good Thing

In addition to providing opportunities for children to be alert for charitable needs in their schools and communities, I think it's wise to give them early opportunities to be competent.

That is, look for ways for them to earn their own money by working. I'm not referring to taking out the trash and the usual household chores, but responsibilities outside the home. This might be mowing lawns, painting fences or anything where they can be in a position of pleasing an employer at an early age. For most of us it's relatively easy just to buy things for our children but they learn a lot by having some "skin in the game."

As they age, it's wise to give them the opportunity to fail. Give them the opportunity to manage a small amount of money and have the experience of knowing what it feels like when it's gone. The concept of managing a small project well before being given a larger project has stood the test of time. Simply providing all of their needs and most of their wants freely while they are under your roof can leave them ill prepared for when they are on their own.

Managing Expectations May Not Come Naturally

Clients have told me that giving cash gifts of $10,000 per year, or whatever the annual gift tax exclusion happens to be, can be addictive to young adult children. They may be tempted to build this into their annual spending plans, which may be fine if the parents are prepared to continue the gifts each year. But, it can be problematic if it becomes difficult for the parents to do so.

Each family is unique, but it's best to begin preparing the heirs early so that they will be experienced and possess the necessary skills to manage assets when the time arrives. Probably the most common approach is for parents to be somewhat secretive, and maintain control while they're alive and then leave it all to their heirs at their death.

Loosening the grip gradually and early seems to work. Personally, I'm a reforming control freak. I'm learning that all I can really control is myself. It's reassuring to know that many of the seeds that we plant may just be dormant for a while. They may not actually emerge and grow until years later, and they may not grow until after we're gone. There's no reason to give up on seeds just because no growth is visible.

Defining the Mission Helps

A few years ago, during a trip to Colorado, our family of five created a family mission statement. We all agreed that we would individually compile a list of the attributes that we wanted our family to possess.

Melissa and I then took the lists and molded them into a statement that included everyone's suggestions. We then arranged for it to be professionally scripted and it's been hanging in a prominent place in our home since. Following are the words that we agreed upon and signed:

The Family Mission

To create a place of faith, love, nurturing
And respect where all five of us are
Encouraged to find and pursue the special
Path of life for which God made us.
To create a happy and peaceful place
Where we give and receive inspiration
And a place of trust where we listen to
Each other and where uniqueness is valued.

Signed this seventh day of January, 1997.

Our family is certainly not perfect, but there's comfort in knowing that other families are not perfect either. We're all works in progress and hopefully are growing with experience. It's almost like the more we know, the more we know we don't know.

Many of our clients are older and their children are often grown. It's common to look back and wonder how things might be different if we had done this or that another way. The fact is, none of us were born with well-developed parenting skills. We learn as we go. Our families are fluid, continually evolving emotional systems with fits and starts and corrections. Along the way, or at the end of the day, there's nothing we can do that changes the past.

However, I'm a big believer that we can change the future and that is best done by changing ourselves first. Failure is a part of life and provides a great way to learn. I think that's a good definition of experience.

By definition, as we grow older, we accumulate more failures and adjustments along the way and this experience becomes valuable. Most of the really big things in life evolve rather slowly such as our habits, personality, values, and most importantly, wisdom.

It's Never Too Late to Take the First Step

In October 1975, Melissa and I bought our first home. It had a large grassy backyard and no trees, and it was within walking distance of my parents' home. One day, I borrowed a shovel and dug up a small oak tree growing on the edge of the woods behind their home. I carried it down the road and dug a hole on

115

the edge of our backyard, and planted the tree. It's a miracle it lived. Now, almost forty years later, when I drive by I can see that tree towering over the backyard.

"The best time to have planted a tree is twenty years ago.
The second best time is today."

– Chinese Proverb

It may have been best to plant a tree twenty years ago. And, twenty years ago may have been the best time to begin a process of grooming the family for the future. But, now can be the second best time to begin. Big and important things may not always happen quickly, but it's never too late to begin.

Leaders are needed along the way to break cycles. It seems to me that the best things seem to happen when there's movement. It may be that progress can be made if we are willing to get outside of our comfort zone.

GENERATIONAL IMPACT

Revealing Our Deepest
Values Is a Worthy Undertaking

Others watch how we handle money as well as relationships. Finding creative ways to demonstrate to the younger generation what's in our hearts and helping them develop empathy for others is valuable. It will help them as they determine who they are on the inside.

AVOIDABLE REGRET

Unclear Family Culture

Most with whom we work are busy and passionate individuals who possess a drive to be productive. Missing the opportunity to help others "see what we see" will be a loss that our successors may not be able to overcome as they assume responsibility for what we leave behind.

EXHIBIT LOVE, INTENTIONALITY, AND WISDOM WITH COMMUNICATION

"Men build too many walls and not enough bridges."

– Sir Isaac Newton

Understanding Others

In 1979, I personally met Stephen Covey before he became famous. He was brought to the home office of an insurance company to speak to a small group of maybe fifteen young insurance guys. I say "guys" because there weren't many females in the business in those days.

The talk was not about how to sell more insurance and I was glad because it focused on something much more important. He talked about human relationships and we each received a copy of a relatively new book of his titled *Spiritual Roots of Human Relations*. I still have the book, although the pages have become somewhat yellowed. I can still visualize Mr. Covey standing in front of that small group, even after all these years, which indicates the deep impression his message left on me.

Habit number five in his best-selling book titled *The 7 Habits of Highly Effective People* is "seek first to understand, then to be understood."[3] That chapter states that communication is the most important skill in life. Seeing things from another's perspective does not often come naturally, but it can be valuable. The yearning to be understood is strong. Sometimes getting outside professional help with relationships is a wise investment.

Relationships between family members and business partners sometimes get off track and complicated. Empathy and communication are usually a part of the remedy that leads to progress. Progress seems to happen when transparency and honesty happen.

There is an exercise that I've seen used successfully in a family and business setting. It's not that complicated, but can be a conversation starter that can lead to both parties understanding of the other's perspective.

First, one individual is asked to write in detail what they want from the business in the future for himself. Then, he is asked to write what he wants the other party to get in the future from the business. The other party is asked to do the same. Afterward, they get together, preferably with a facilitator, to discuss. An understanding of each other's perspective, desires, and dreams is deepened. Empathy should be enhanced.

---

[3] Stephen Covey, *The 7 Habits of Highly Effective People,* (New York: Free Press, 2004).

A Business Surprise

One of our business clients is a successful distributor of specialty products. The business was founded by two brothers, Fred and Wayne. Fred owned 70 percent and Wayne owned 30 percent.

Fred, who owned 70 percent of the business, passed away suddenly about twenty years ago. There was an agreement in place that required Wayne to purchase Fred's 70 percent interest from the estate. The agreement was funded with life insurance. It was a great plan and it worked beautifully, but the missing link in the plan was that Fred had never mentioned the plan to his wife, Patricia, now his widow.

Fred's unexpected death occurred midweek, and the funeral was on a Friday. On Monday morning, Wayne received a call indicating that Patricia would arrive at the office early that afternoon. In the meantime, Fred's office was off-limits and no one was to enter. When Patricia arrived, incorrectly assuming that she was the new majority owner of the business, she began to call employees into "her" office for interviews about future plans for the business.

The firm's attorney had to be called in to review the buy/sell agreement. This was a surprise to Fred's family as they were cashed out of the business. Patricia had difficulty coping with the multiple transitions underway. She lost her husband of many years. She was no longer connected to the business that was their security. She was wondering what her future life would be like.

She received an ample amount of cash and the plan was most appropriate, but the sudden transitions were difficult. Fred's lack of communication about the plan and the reasons for it caused pain. Hearing about the structure of the business buy out from the attorney, whom Patricia had never met, was awkward at best. From a relationship standpoint, negative surprises rarely turn out well.

Hindsight indicates that the business would not have grown and prospered, and in fact may not even exist today, had the buy/sell agreement not been in place and funded. Suddenly inserting a new and unqualified personality into the ownership structure of a business rarely works out well.

Regret That Could Have Been Avoided

- No communication of the business succession plan created stress and relationship strain

Keeping Everyone in the Dark Is a Bad Plan

Anyone who has had to manage the affairs for a parent without a power of attorney or health care directive, or settled an estate where the decedent did not have a valid will, wants his own family to avoid such a time consuming and unpleasant experience. Similarly, searching through drawers and files in a deceased person's home trying to find documents, bank accounts, and insurance policies can be a stressful experience. Those who have had to do that are most likely inclined to organize, in some fashion, their own personal affairs.

For example, there have been occasions where we've been asked to sort through a box of old insurance policies and determine which ones may still be in effect so that claims may be pursued. There is a propensity to keep old insurance policies and other financial documents even after they are no longer valid.

A friend told me that his ninety-year-old father maintained control of everything until he died and did no estate planning. His financial records and leases on rental properties were in disarray. In addition to all the financial records that had to be found and sorted, $1.5 million of estate taxes had to be paid in cash within nine months.

I knew this elderly gentleman personally. I know that he did not intend to exit this world and leave such a painful experience for his son, but it happened anyway. It's hard to know why.

It may be that when he settled the estates of his own parents years ago, the process was simple. Most likely, they had few financial assets and dividing up the personal effects between he and his siblings was fairly simple. Along the way, my friend's father and mother acquired significant assets and complexity, but they never felt particularly wealthy.

It's awkward to talk with your children about your impending demise. It's even more awkward for the adult children to bring it up and ask for disclosure about accumulated assets and financial documents. After all, these details may have been kept private for several decades. Unfortunately, the last generation's way of planning and estate settlement won't work well in today's complex world.

A Family Meeting

As human beings, it's okay if we acknowledge that we will not live on this earth forever. It's understandable that it's not a particularly fun subject because dying and all things associated with passing on seem so final. Nevertheless, it is healthy to transparently acknowledge the inevitable. In my world, it's called planning and being prepared.

The vision of simply living hard and fast, then one day disappearing, and leaving those you love the most in any sort of confusion, seems unsightly at best.

We are advocates of periodic family meetings. The degree of transparency around specifics related to asset values and so forth will depend on each situation. We feel that these meetings should be in a business oriented setting and include a printed agenda distributed in advance. Here is an example:

Agenda

Initial Family Meeting - December 1, 5:30 PM
Purpose of Meeting - Mom and Dad
Review of Family Mission Statement - Mom
Family Financial Philosophy - Mom and Dad
Overview of Planning Documents - Dad
  • Power of Attorney
  • Health Care Directive
  • Irrevocable Trust
  • Wills
Specific bequests for personal property
  • Revocable Trust
Conceptual Diagram of Current Estate Plan - Dad
Creation of Family Foundation - Mom and Dad
Dinner/Discussion

The purpose of the meeting is to promote strong family relations and anticipate future concerns related to material possessions. The initial thought of this may make some uncomfortable. But in the end, there will be some version of a family meeting—with the older generation present, or not. In other words, it will happen with us or without us. The meeting may be after we're gone. It's best if the meeting happens while the parent, or parents, can participate. If we don't explain our actions, someone else will have to do so.

It's even better if these meetings are held periodically, with the parents present, so the family can benefit from their presence, reasons, and logic. If the only meeting happens in the lawyer's office after the parents are gone, their absence will be felt.

The need for communication is critical regardless of the estate size. I've heard it said that some people spend forty years accumulating wealth, twenty years trying to preserve it, and about forty minutes deciding how it will be dispensed when they are gone.

Whatever the makeup or value of the property, most would prefer that it not be a vehicle to create disharmony. Our legacy will not be impacted by what we intended to do, only by what we did. It's doubtful that a surprise will end up being positive. It's best to be as transparent as possible. The family can see that the parents have put a lot of thought into the plan and have tried hard to get it right. It's important to point out that the plan may change so that expectations are managed.

It's wise to review at least conceptually the estate plan along with the flow of assets into various trusts and the reason for the structure. It's often wise to include at least one member of the advisory team that's familiar with the plan, perhaps the attorney, to help explain the provisions.

Relationships that grow around common experiences are the greatest asset any family can possess. Most people would trade anything for the treasure of experiencing authentic, loving exchanges with family members. The trip will be worth the effort.

A Road to Generational Connection

The Ultimate Gift is one of the best books I've ever read on the subject of generational connection and impact. The book is a novel written by Jim Stovall.[4] It's a story about a wealthy grandfather trying his best to convey twelve life lessons to his grandson. The story is woven around a series of videos created by the grandfather prior to his death. The book is about hands-on learning in order for the grandson to see what the grandfather had come to see in his later years.

I believe the older generation has a lot inside themselves that they would like to share about what they've learned and experienced. More often than not, it is mostly kept inside and I'm not sure why this happens. Perhaps it's the fear of being misunderstood, judged, not having the right words, or maybe it's baggage from the past. But, for whatever reason, much is left unsaid in important relationships.

I also believe the younger generation is not inclined to coax information out of their elders because there's a feeling that the

---

[4] Jim Stovall, *The Ultimate Gift,* (Dallas: Executive Books, 2000).

elders will always be around. Curiosity about our ancestor's lives and experiences sometimes happens after it's too late.

Advances in technology are simplifying the process of creating and preserving personal stories. A growing practice is that of creating a video that includes the older generation sharing stories about what they have learned and observed during their lifetimes. The value of this cannot be overstated. Seeds sown along the way may take years to germinate and in fact may blossom after were gone.

Most likely, the younger generation will have to ask their elders to sit for this project. In doing so, it will honor their life and to some degree put a face and voice on a lifetime of experience.

Family Stories from the Heart

Being in the business I'm in has helped develop in me a strong belief that relationships and the experience of being connected with others is a huge contributing factor to happiness. I wish I knew more about my ancestors. I'd like to know more about what their lives were like, what they thought about, and so forth.

That's why a few years ago, I decided to start writing periodic "one pagers" about whatever happened to be on my mind at the time along with whatever I may be learning at the time. We're all continuing works in progress. For me, writing down and communicating my thoughts is a way of passing along what's in my heart to following generations. A picture is worth a thousand words, so below is an example:

Dear David, Jonathan, and Laura:

"The Lord himself goes before you and will be with you; he will never leave you nor forsake you. Do not be afraid; do not be discouraged."

– Deuteronomy 31:8

Security Life of Denver owned a large condominium in Vail, Colorado, and in the early 1990s, they arranged for us to stay in it for a week during the middle of the winter. This was one of the best trips I recall us taking because the place was so beautiful and the snow was so deep. David and Jonathan enjoyed the skiing and the speed and the thrill of going downhill fast. I don't recall exactly, but Laura was probably five or six years old at the time. I spent a lot of time with her.

One afternoon, Laura and I were near the top of the mountain, and the snow began to fall quite heavily. The guy running the ski lift indicated that they were in the process of closing the mountain because of the heavy snow. As Laura and I began to descend the mountain, we found ourselves in the middle of a "white out." The visibility was practically zero. Since I'm not particularly good at observing signs anyway, we somehow found ourselves on an isolated and very steep slope. I noticed that no one else was around. We were alone.

As anybody that has ever been snow skiing knows, it's difficult to turn around and go back uphill, so the only choice was to keep going down. Laura was following me and slightly up the hill behind me. She slid off into the woods, and her skis came off so I had to stop and take my skis off in order to retrieve her. From this point, I was carrying four skis as we trudged downhill.

By now, I'm starting to get worried about our predicament since we were essentially lost and alone on a big mountain in a white out. The significant part of this experience was how calm Laura remained. After all, she was with her father so there was nothing to worry about. She was actually enjoying the snow. On the inside, I started remembering stories of how people sometimes get lost on mountains and have to spend the night in the snow. Nevertheless, I was reassuring to her and did not panic. All I knew was that going downhill was good. Finally, a lift station became visible downhill and we were able to make our way down the mountain.

A significant take away from this for me was how calm and peaceful Laura was because she was with her father. She was totally dependent on me and completely fine with that. Secondly, because of my love for her, I recall my primary purpose was to keep her close to me, protect her, and above all else not let her get lost in the snow.

I'm grateful that I am blessed to be an earthly father. It helps me better understand God's love for me (and you).

Love,

Dad

A certain amount of transparency is required with healthy relationships, but this may not come naturally. Many significant things happen when we are out of our comfort zone. Missing the opportunity to intentionally express how we feel about our most important relationships will be a huge loss to all who follow.

GENERATIONAL IMPACT

Committing to Communication Expresses Love

Maturity is required in order to acknowledge that our time on earth will end, and others that we care about deeply will remain. This maturity and transparency deepens relationships, and the experience will affect those who follow. Being intentional makes a statement about the heart.

AVOIDABLE REGRET

Inadequate Communication

Deep emotions that are not communicated leave mystery and uncertainty that can be painful for those who follow.

PART III

A PLACE TO BEGIN

OUR LIFE INSURANCE PLANNING PROCESS

"Try not to become a person of success, but rather to become a person of value. He who is considered successful in our day gets more out of life than he puts in. But a person of value will give more than he receives."

– Albert Einstein

As stated in the beginning, life insurance planning is a specialty of our firm. And, as noted previously, there are other members of the advisory planning team. Each member of the team will have a structured process oriented toward helping the client accomplish their objectives. Each member wants to create value for their client and have their own way to create that experience.

For example, from the life insurance planning standpoint, we have created a six-step process that serves as a framework to accomplish the individual objectives of our clients.

Our six-step process, summarized on the following page, varies based upon the situation, and has served our clients well over the years.

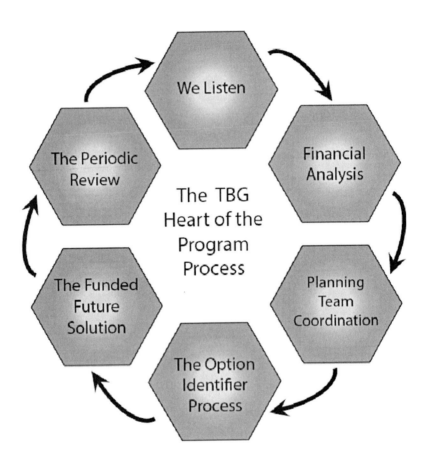

We Listen

Financial Analysis

The Periodic Review

The TBG Heart of the Program Process

Planning Team Coordination

The Funded Future Solution

The Option Identifier Process

STEP

1

We Listen

I believe this is the most important step. The more we listen and learn about our client, the more we are able to help.

We think through and identify concerns and dangers that are present. We want to understand what needs to happen over the next duration of time in order for us to feel good about the progress.

A great place to begin is with this question: "If we were having a discussion one year from now, and you were looking back over the past twelve months, what has to have happened, from an estate planning standpoint, for you to feel good about our progress?"

Another question we might ask is, "If a death or disability occurs, what needs to happen? What is the vision of what the aftermath needs to look like?" Part of this process is to walk into the future and take a look at family financial concerns, business concerns and other issues that may be present.

Financial Needs Analysis

Based upon the conversation in Step 1, we would create a list of facts and documents that we need. This might include a financial statement and present insurance contracts.

With the policy owner's authorization, we would request updated projections and values for each life insurance policy that's in place.

For business owners, we would need details related to any buy/sell agreements and succession plans that are in place.

Then, based upon the information that is been assembled, we would prepare some preliminary projections for the present situation as well as a solution that we might propose.

STEP

3

Planning Team Coordination

In our role, we do not practice law or give tax advice, but our clients need someone in their lives, with whom they have a relationship, who does practice law and give tax advice. It's best if a team is in place.

If a team doesn't exist, we can certainly assist with the creation of one. Often we find that our clients have outgrown their relationships and a second opinion is desired. For example, if the current legal documents have not been reviewed in a while, a decision has to be made with regard to who should perform the review. That is, the original attorney who drafted the documents, or someone new?

STEP

4

The Option Identifier Process

Our process for the acquisition of life insurance is comprehensive. Typically, the first step is to obtain our client's authorization to submit their medical history to several insurance carriers. We submit these records electronically and we are not applying for insurance at this stage. We are merely asking the carriers for an "informal" offer with regard to an underwriting classification.

The underwriting classification has a significant effect upon the rates. The classification could be "preferred," "standard," or some higher and more costly rating such as a "Table C or D." The higher we go up the alphabet, the higher the rates go as we approach becoming uninsurable. We often request responses from ten or fifteen major insurance companies, and once we have the preliminary offers we negotiate among the leading contenders.

Next, we consider the financial ratings of the various insurance companies and the type of insurance that is most appropriate for our client. It is interesting that most carriers have "sweet spots." For example, one company might be competitive for younger applicants and non-competitive for older individuals. Another insurance company might take the opposite position. Our ability to work with many insurance companies provides significant value to our clients.

Once we have the preliminary underwriting offer, we are able to prepare some solutions for our client to consider. It's at this stage that we review the appropriateness of any life insurance presently in effect. Sometimes it's best to maintain the current coverage. However, it may be advantageous to exchange existing policies for new ones based upon the facts involved.

The comparison we create includes details provided by the present insurance company on the current coverage in effect. The facts, figures, and projections are obtained directly from the present insurance carriers after we provide authorization from the policy owner.

The Funded Future Solution

There are really five fundamental decisions that have to be made regarding life insurance. First, how much insurance is needed now? Second, how might the need change in the future? Third, how long does the insurance need to last? Forth, how important are guarantees? And fifth, what is the risk profile of the policy owner? We have a process designed to help our clients think through these issues.

At this stage, we compare options based upon the preliminary underwriting offers that we have negotiated among the various insurance companies. A decision is then made to proceed and applications are submitted. We are believers in diversification, so we may suggest that the coverage be divided among two or more different insurance companies.

After the formal offer is confirmed and the policy is issued, the coverage is then placed into effect.

STEP

6

The Periodic Review

After any new legal documents have been executed, and any new insurance has been placed into effect, a feeling of satisfaction is usually experienced. Everything is organized and tucked away.

Nevertheless, the planning process is an evolving project, and we believe it's best to think through the question of how often we wish to have a review. Our recommendation is that plans should be reviewed annually, but the frequency is up to the client. This would include a review of the performance of any products involved and an update related to personal objectives as life evolves.

CONCLUSION

"Grace is the face that love wears,
when it meets imperfection."

– Joseph R. Cooke

E state planning at its core is about relationships. You might say, "Wait a minute, isn't it really about my property?" Yes, it's about property, but the property isn't yours anymore because we are planning for after you're gone.

What was once your property, possibly along with some liabilities and unfinished responsibilities, is now in the hands of others. Without a well thought out, best effort plan for this transitional phase—including communication to those involved—disharmony and financial hardship may result. Being prepared, and having no regrets at this point is a worthy objective.

I believe the most critical challenges families face are rarely financial. They are relationship based. Therefore, I believe that being intentional about relationships is wise.

Being intentional means having a target. One of my sons, Jonathan, is a commercial airline pilot. He earned his private pilot license while he was in high school. Not long after he received his license, he invited me to fly with him one Saturday afternoon. As we were sitting at the end of the runway, he began adjusting the dials on the instrument panel. I asked what he was doing and he said, "We're going to Murphy, North Carolina."

Because of the plane's onboard navigation system, we made it to that small airport in the mountains and back, even though the winds and other factors blew us off course from time to time. The guidance system knew where we wanted to go, and it remained focused upon our destination.

During the period of time that this book was being written, my father passed away. My world is different from the world that he and his father knew. Navigation systems have been created because we want to arrive at a desired destination, and want a system that will assist during the journey. From a personal, relationship, and financial standpoint, each generation navigates through a period of time that has issues unique to it.

Some things change; some things don't change. Some sort of guidance system is essential. One thing that doesn't change, I believe, is that smooth-running relationships between individuals rarely if ever happen by accident. "Getting it right" rarely happens without intentional effort.

I've experienced family members entering this world and I've experienced family members leaving this world. These experiences have changed me.

The Rev. F. Washington Jarvis writes in his book, *With Love and Prayers,*

> Important, though, as a vision is (regarding career and lifestyle), it is nothing like as important as an overall vision for your whole life. We might call such a vision existential; it has to do with the discovery by you of some meaning and purpose to your whole existence.

Inevitably such a vision must entail not only finding meaning in your life but meaning also in your inevitable death.[5]

He goes on to say, "If you want to be happy, you must learn to love, and pay the price of caring for others, of putting them first, often inconveniencing yourself. That is the pathway to happiness."

In the beginning of this book, I shared a little of my family's story. The Epilogue that follows gives some insight into the rest of the story, and the ongoing progress underway.

---

[5] F. Washington Jarvis, *With Love and Prayers*, (Boston: David R. Godine, 2010).

Thoughts Delivered by Gary Bottoms
at His Father's Funeral

February 2, 2013

L ast Tuesday morning at eight thirty, the Lord said, "It's time, bring him home." Since then, as you would expect, I've thought a lot about my dad's life and our relationship and I'd like to reflect a little on some things that I think he would want me to say at this moment.

First, a little background: eight years ago, my sister Judy and I moved our parents from their home to an assisted living facility. As a lot of you know, our mother died about five and half years ago, afflicted with Alzheimer's disease. So, five and half years ago, I stood here and said to my dad who was sitting here on the front row, "We need you." I had not planned to say that, and I didn't know at the time how we might need him.

The entire family has walked down this road with my parents and for the last five years with our dad alone who was also afflicted with Alzheimer's disease. The experience has changed me and I needed that. We have all learned a lot, and I'd like to share just a little of what I've learned personally.

1. **I have a new perspective about the future.**

The weekend before last, Melissa and I were keeping Drew, our grandson, because David and Brittney were out of town. And, my dad took a turn for the worse. I spent a lot of time that weekend with my dad and I thought a lot about the cycle of life.

Fifteen-month-old Drew is bright, energetic and happy and his life is just beginning, and I contrasted that with my dad who had seemingly slipped away. I thought about how in my earlier years going through school and so forth, I really didn't give much thought to heaven or that life here could be limited because aging seemed so far away. During my middle years that were so busy, I didn't give much thought to it either because becoming older seemed so distant. Now, having spent eight years in and around assisted living and memory units, the experience has changed me.

I sat around the memory unit two weeks ago today, and stared into the mostly blank faces of people who once had schedules and responsibilities and dreams for the future, but are now mostly passive and quiet and need help with most everything. I thought about the future for them, and for me.

The good news is that, if they are believers, they have a very big and very bright future for all of eternity in heaven. That's the way a loving God—in all of his wisdom—planned it; the present is only a short transitional phase and the best is yet to come. What's about to end is not that much of a big deal compared to what is about to begin.

> "For I know the plans I have for you," declares the Lord, "plans to prosper you and not to harm you, plans to give you hope and a future."
>
> – Jeremiah 29:11

The future is way beyond what we can see or comprehend.

2. **I have a new perspective on what home is all about.**

I used to think of home as a structure and a physical place, but that is changed. A few days ago, I was standing in the hallway speaking with a hospice nurse and a sweet little lady walked up to me and said, "Sir, will you please take me home?" As some of you know, Alzheimer's patients frequently ask to be taken home.

Eight years ago, my mother started asking about going home. They do that because where they are just doesn't feel right, and they want to go to another place that feels better than where they are.

As believers, we know about heaven, and believe in it, but I can say personally that up until recent years I had not given it that much thought. I haven't heard many sermons on the subject. I became so interested in heaven that I read a 500-page book that referenced lots of scripture related to heaven and the continuation of our existence. That's significant because I don't read many thick books, especially if they have small print.

After reading the book, and thinking more about it, my understanding of what home is really about changed.

My dad and my mom both understood this and their passion was working with the Gideons International. [Reference Gideon Bibles] Inside the worn covers of the two Bibles I'm holding are 206 handwritten dates with churches noted all over Georgia where my dad spoke telling the Gideon story.

He raised a lot of funds to help distribute Bibles, and was called "the Bible Man" by the folks at the motels up and down Highway 41. I didn't know that until recently. I'm proud of him for doing that. Traveling the state and speaking at 206 Sunday services indicated an intentional commitment.

The Bible is a lot of things, but to sum it up for me at this moment, it's a guidebook to home. I was present when my grandmother died, that's my dad's mother. I was there with my dad, my mom, and my dad's brother and sister, and I remember my dad saying just after his mother took her last breath that there's a happy reunion taking place. I remember that moment well but in the last few years, I've come to understand it better.

Last Tuesday morning, as Melissa and I were beside my dad's bed, I noticed some photographs on the wall and the photographs were of my two grandmothers, my great-grandmother, and my mom and dad, and I mentioned that they are all in heaven now.

So as we get older, things begin to tilt, that is, more of the significant people in our lives have gone on to eternity. During the younger years, most everyone is still with you. This life, that we in this room have now, is just a small little dot on the line compared to all of eternity. This seems a little mysterious, but that's the way God, in his perfect wisdom, planned it.

> "As you do not know the path of the wind, or how the body is formed in a mother's womb, so you cannot understand the work of God, the Maker of all things."
>
> – Ecclesiastes 11:5

There's a lot we can't figure out—it's mysterious.

3. **I have a new perspective on relationships.**

During recent years, on my dad's good days, we had some very meaningful conversations. One of the most meaningful was about three weeks ago, just before my dad went into a steep decline. I actually made a video of part of the conversation with my phone and I circulated it to our family.

My dad was pointing to pictures on the wall and saying how proud he was of his family. He saw the picture of my mother and asked, "Where's Mary?" I said, "Mary died about five years ago...she's in heaven."

He just sat there for a few moments and said, "I love Mary."

I asked what he was going to do when he finds her in heaven and he said, "I'm going to hug her neck."

Then I asked what he was going to tell her and he said, "I'm going tell her I love her," and added that they were "going to get married."

My dad had a good sense of humor, and for some reason, I said, "I'm not sure you can marry in heaven."

He quickly replied, "I think we'll be able to work that out." The Bottoms bloodline doesn't readily accept that something can't be done.

So my dad is now where he wanted to be. He was ready. In fact, he was ready a long time ago.

I said when I first started that my dad went home last Tuesday morning at about eight thirty. It's no coincidence that exactly one week before that, on the previous Tuesday around eight thirty, I stopped by Greenwood Gardens and it was breakfast time. I fed him his breakfast because he could not feed himself and he could not communicate. I think that may have been the last solid food meal that he actually ate.

It was part of God's plan for me that I stop by that morning, because after breakfast I was standing in front of him in his wheelchair, and he started speaking and I heard some words. I heard him say, "The Lord's going to take me." I wasn't sure I heard that correctly and I leaned over and asked if he could say that again and he said, "The Lord is going to take me, and I'm sorry I've caused y'all so much trouble."

I said, "You haven't caused us any trouble at all and I'm very proud of you and I love you very much."

He said, "I love you, too." Those were the last words I heard him say. He then slipped back into his uncommunicative state.

This is not a sad story. It's a story about an incredible life and that my dad made a significant place for the Lord in his heart. Many father-son relationships have baggage, but I can say that whatever baggage was there has evaporated for me. For me, that's important.

The memories are precious but the future is glorious. God's grace and the wonder of his plan for us is amazing.

"I have fought the good fight, I have finished the race, I have kept the faith."

– 2 Timothy 4:7

BIBLIOGRAPHY

Jarvis, F. Washington. *With Love and Prayers*. Boston: David R. Godine, 2010.

Hughes, James. *Family Wealth—Keeping it in the Family*. Hoboken, NJ: Bloomberg, 2004.

Covey, Stephen. *The 7 Habits of Highly Effective People*. New York: Free Press, 2004.

SUGGESTED READING

Aronoff, PhD, Craig, and John Ward, PhD. *Family Meetings: How to Build a Stronger Family and a Stronger Business*. Marietta, GA: Family Enterprise Publishers, 2002.

Blouin, Barbara, and Katherine Gibson. *The Legacy of Inherited Wealth*. New York: Trio Press, 1995.

Blue, Ron. *Splitting Heirs*. Chicago: Northfield Publishing, 2004.

Brown, John. *Cash Out Move On*. Denver: Business Enterprise Press, 2008.

Brown, John. *How to Run Your Business So You Can Leave It In Style*. Denver: Business Enterprise Press, 1993.

Buford, Bob. *Half Time*. Grand Rapids, MI: Zondervan Publishing House, 2008.

Burkett, Larry. *Preparing for Retirement*. Chicago: Moody Press, 1992.

Carnegie, Andrew. *The Gospel of Wealth Essays and Other Writings*. Bedford, MA: Applewood Books, 1998.

Collier, Charles. *Wealth in Families*. Boston: Harvard University, 2012.

Covey, Stephen. *Spiritual Roots of Human Relations*. Salt Lake City: Deseret Book Company, 1970.

Covey, Stephen. *The 7 Habits of Highly Effective Families*. New York: Golden Books, 1997.

Cullman, Lewis. *Can't Take it With You*. Hoboken, NJ: John Wiley & Sons, 2004.

Danco, Leon. *Beyond Survival*. Upper Saddle River, NJ: Reston Publishing Co., 2003.

Eldredge, John. *Wild at Heart*. Nashville: Thomas Nelson Publishers, 2011.

Frankl, Viktor. *Man's Search for Meaning*. Boston: Beacon Press, 1959.

Hausner, Lee. *Children of Paradise*. Los Angeles: Jeremy P. Tarcher, 1990.

Hughes, James. *Family Wealth*. Hoboken, NJ: Bloomberg Press, 2004.

Inside the Minds. *Family and Business Succession Planning Strategies*. New York: Thomas Reuters Westlaw, 2012.

Jordan, Joseph. *Living a Life of Significance*. Bryn Mawr, PA: The American College Press, 2013.

Keller, Timothy. *The Prodigal God*. New York: Dutton, 2008.

Lansberg, Ivan. *Succeeding Generations*. Boston: Harvard Business School Press, 1999.

MacDonald, Gordon. *Secrets of the Generous Life*. Carol Stream, IL: Tyndale House Publishers, 2002.

Maister, David, Charles Green, and Robert Galford. *The Trusted Advisor*. New York: Touchstone, 2000.

O'Kelly, Eugene. *Chasing Daylight*. New York: McGraw-Hill, 2005.

Scazzero, Peter. *Emotionally Healthy Spirituality*. Nashville: Thomas Nelson, 2003.

Schon, Donald. *The Reflective Practitioner*. New York: Basic Books, 1983.

Sinek, Simon. *Start With Why*. New York: Portfolio/ Penguin, 2009.

Sonnenfeld, Jeffrey. *The Hero's Farewell*. New York: Oxford University Press, 1988.

Steadman, Ray. *Is This All There Is To Life?* Colorado Springs, CO: Multnomah Books, 1998.

Stovall, Jim. *The Ultimate Gift*. Colorado Springs, CO: David C. Cook, 2003.

Thrall, Bill, Bruce McNicol, and John Lynch. *TrueFaced*. Colorado Springs, CO: NavPress, 2003.

Ware, Bronnie. *The Top Five Regrets of the Dying*. Carlsbad, CA: Hay House, 2012.

Williams, Roy, and Vic Preisser. *Philanthropy Heirs & Values*. Brandon, OR: Robert D. Reed Publishers, 2005.

Gary Bottoms is President of The Bottoms Group, LLC. He is a graduate of the Georgia Institute of Technology. He also holds the Chartered Life Underwriter designation and the Chartered Financial Consultant designation from the American College.

He entered the financial services industry in 1975, specialized in insurance. His extensive experience and human relations skills have been developed over the years working with professional, high net worth and corporate clients across the United States. His passion for serving others is evidenced by a history of professional and community involvement.

Professional Involvement

- A past president of the Atlanta Association of Insurance and Financial Advisors. From this organization, he received the Harry I. Davis Award, which is given to one member annually who represents the highest ideals and principles of the financial services profession.

- A member of the Association for Advanced Life Underwriting, which is an invitation only organization, composed of life insurance professionals serving the high-end marketplace. For this group, he serves as a key liaison with two members of the United States Senate.

- A past board member of the Atlanta Estate Planning Council and past president of the North Georgia Estate Planning Council.

Community Involvement

- Served as the Board Chairman of the Cobb Community Foundation, the Cobb Schools Foundation, the WellStar Health System Foundation, the Center for Family Resources, and President of the Rotary Club of Marietta.

- A former member of the Board of Trustees of the Georgia Tech Alumni Association receiving the Volunteer of the Year Award.

- Graduate of Leadership Georgia and has been involved in numerous other civic, church and community endeavors, and was selected as the 2012 Marietta Citizen of the Year.

Gary and his wife, Melissa, have been married since 1975. They live in Marietta, Georgia.